Sole Sisters

The Joys and Pains
of Single Black Women

Deborah Mathis

A Bolden Book

AGATE

CHICAGO

Bolden Books is an imprint of Agate Publishing, Inc.

Printed in Canada.

Library of Congress Cataloging-in-Publication Data

Mathis, Deborah.
    Sole sisters : the joys and pains of single Black women / Deborah Mathis.
        p.   cm.
    "A Bolden book."
    Summary: "Examines the reasons behind and implications of remaining single as a Black woman"— Provided by publisher.
    ISBN-13: 978-1-932841-27-5 (pbk.)
    ISBN-10: 1-932841-27-X (pbk.)
    1. Single women—United States—Psychology.   2. African American women—Psychology.   3. African American single people—Psychology.   4. Interpersonal relations—United States. 5. Man-woman relationships—United States.   I. Title.
    HQ800.2.M37 2007
    306.815308996073—dc22

                                      2007007459

12 11 10 09 08 07   10 9 8 7 6 5 4 3 2 1

Agate books are available in bulk at discount prices. For more information, go to agatepublishing.com.

Dedication

For Love and Faith and Hope.

Acknowledgements

As always, I am indebted to my family for allowing me to hibernate with my computer for long spells. When I would emerge disheveled, disoriented, and, invariably, needy, my children kept my ego and spirits fed with constant, florid words of encouragement. I often felt overwhelmed and wished aloud I had never learned to read and write, but their support always bolstered me.

My sister and her family in Orlando ran my errands, took me away from it all occasionally, and never made me feel like a burden. My mother and stepfather opened their home to me for nine long months and allowed me to work in a peaceful room with sunshine and flowers just outside my window. They fed me and loved me, sweetening the pot with smiles that never once drooped or faded. My brothers and their families checked in every now and then to ask how I was doing and to express their pride and faith in me anew. God showed out when He gave me this bunch.

I am also grateful to my trusty friend and former agent, Caroline F. Carney, who went ga-ga over this project and stayed with me despite my missed deadlines and bouts of malaise and hysteria.

In particular, I want to thank my daughter, Allison, who painstakingly re-typed the manuscript for me after the disk went missing and I almost lost my mind.

I'll never be able to repay what I owe to the many women who opened their hearts and memory banks to me, who pushed into the pain instead of pulling away, and who helped me laugh at myself, study myself, and find solace in the sisterhood of single black women. I hope I've done them justice. They deserve some of that.

Contents

❀

Foreword

How're We Doin'?

ONE MORNING, I dressed in ragged sweatpants and a mismatched shirt and hobbled the trash cans to the curb. As I did, I wondered what my mostly married neighbors were thinking of me. Did they laugh when the lid of one can popped off, and a week's worth of eggs cartons, apples cores, chicken bones and pantyhose wrappers tumbled onto the lawn … which, by the way, I used to mow myself until I gave in and hired a lawn service? Did they tsk-tsk behind their blinds and pity me for having to do so much of the heavy lifting? Maybe a few thought, "What a woman!" Maybe they had some admiration for me for having the energy and know-how to get so much done on my own … even changing a flat tire, which I can do, you know.

For a moment, I even felt a little sorry for myself, and felt like boo-hooing about my predicament, which, alas, entails much more than spilled garbage. But I quickly collected myself and felt pretty proud that I'm doing it all on my own. It was too cold out there to worry about what anyone thinks or what any of that meant right then.

The truck was coming. And there went that damn lid again! My back was killing me. I thought, "To hell with woman's liberation, my independence, and all that jazz. A man is supposed to be taking out my trash. And I don't mean my son. Women with men in their lives don't have this problem, do they?"

When I was growing up in the South in the '50s and '60s, everybody was married. My parents. Their parents. Their brothers and sisters and cousins and aunts and uncles. The family friends. The folks across the street, up the street, down the street, and next door. My teachers. The woman who fixed our hair. Our doctors and dentists. Occasionally, you'd come across a woman in her prime who was unmarried, but she'd be the tragic widow or the rare divorcée who had to manage her own needs and desires and at the same time keep the community gossips at bay as they monitored her comings and goings. Any de-flowered, full-grown woman on the loose was trouble, for sure.

Most of the unmarried women of marriageable age were barely women, such as the college coeds who babysat us when our parents were out for the evening. The other unattached women were the ingénues at church, with fresh, smooth skin and shapely bodies. We knew it was only a matter of time before they did what all young women did and made a trip down some kind of aisle with some kind of man.

Every now and then, the grown-ups would start whispering about one of these pretty young misses. Once the buzz got started, we nosy youngsters would quickly figure out the girl was probably "in trouble." It was often a lass who had grown faint in the choir loft or nauseated in Sunday school. Her waist might be noticeably thicker, her hair might have dramatically changed in length or texture, and she might appear at church in billowy blouses—or stop going altogether.

Usually, that young woman would eventually end up standing be-side the baby's father with flowers in her hand, a hat on her head, and a brand new ring on her finger. When no marriage occurred for the expectant young woman, it usually meant the new mother and her child would be living with her parents and waiting for the baby's father to come around, which was presumed—or hoped, at least—to be an eventuality. When conscience, reason, and appeals to family honor failed, some families weren't above harassing or shaming the fellow. In those days, and in that part of the country, if you made a baby, you'd better get ready to make a wedding too, even if you were too young, not really in love, and had no visible means of supporting yourself, let alone a wife and child. It was better to have an illogical, all-odds-against-it, premature, and rocky marriage than none at all.

Sometimes the rumor mill would imply that a girl had "went and gotten herself pregnant" as a means of trapping a man into marriage. That was certainly a rumor that a gossip would have no way of verifying and about which she had no business speculating, to be sure. Besides, if it were true, it was certainly a dangerous gamble. Despite the pressure to "do the right thing," young men still frequently defied the altar's call. This was considered immoral, irresponsible, and cavalier behavior, and sometimes enough scorn and repudiation from the community would turn the guy around. But sometimes not.

Getting married was simply expected of people, and young women bore the brunt of this cultural demand. Back then, the terms "spinster" and "old maid" were still alive and well, and many young women dreaded of the stigma of becoming identified primarily by her unmarried state at the tender age of 25. She'd have to abide rude questions and curious looks about why she "couldn't get a man."

Time changed that. I was in junior high when I started hearing of it—equality for women and men. I was immediately drawn to the idea because it fit my own ambitions. My mother was both an excellent homemaker and an excellent professional educator, so the demand for woman's equality sounded like long-overdue justice to me.

However, since I'd spent the formative years of my life under the old paradigm, the marriage idea remained part of my plan. To me, the women's rights movement meant I'd get an extension of the deadline for getting hitched. The stigma associated with single womanhood would get moved to a later stage in life—say, the mid-30s, rather than the mid-20s.

I also latched on to the movement's other "benefit": the concept of the "50-50" marriage, where husband and wife equally shared responsibilities and kept the marriage, the family, and the household running smoothly together.

So much for that theory. Here I am—divorced, with 100 percent of the work and none of the good stuff like sex, companionship, financial support, and someone to take the trash out on cold Monday mornings. The truth is, it's not all that bad, this being single. It certainly isn't the kind of thing that people whisper about anymore. Doing so would be a full-time job these days, since single black women are the norm.

. . .

The storied man-woman imbalance may not be as pronounced elsewhere as in the nation's capital, but the laws of supply and demand would leave us empty-handed in just about any American city south of Nome. Remember that song by the Weather Girls, "It's Raining Men"? Well, it's looking like a drought now, my sisters. It's reflected in the unprecedented number of unattached black women. According to the 2000 U.S. Census, there are more than 14 million unmarried black females in the United States, and only a little more than 4 million of our sisters are married. There are fewer than 14 million people—men, women, boys, and girls—in all of Chile or Cambodia. Only four U.S. states have populations of more than 14 million people.

Some sociologists, psychologists, and anthropologists have said the very institution of marriage is on the rocks in black America. They consider it to be a "crisis." Individual black women may beg to differ, since many are quite content to be single and have made a conscious decision to become or remain so. These women are not accidents or demographic disparities.

Personal contentment notwithstanding, when a seismic shift occurs in the way black people live, the implications for the future of black America can hardly be shrugged off.

This is a new predicament. In the 1950s, most black adults were married, as 62 percent of black women and 64 percent of black men were legally partnered. Only about one-third of either gender was unhitched, and most of them were divorced or widowed. The smallest group was the "never-marrieds."

As the 20th century proceeded, the married and unmarried numbers began to even out. In 1980, for the first time in our nearly 400 years on these shores, single black women in the U.S. outnumbered married black women. Today, the 1950s norm has been turned on its ear, and most black adults are unmarried. Forty percent of black women have never been married.

There are myriad reasons for these changes in black American marriage trends: educational, cultural, political, psychological, and sexual reasons, to name a few. Economics and health trends certainly play roles as well. But all of these factors have a common bottom line: a shortage of marriageable black men.

This imbalance starts in the womb. Worldwide, there are more females born than males. "For every 100 black women living, there are 85 black men," according to the U.S. Census Bureau. The Census Bureau starts the count of "women" and "men" at age 15. However, when you begin your search at age 18—the commonly accepted and legal age of majority—the gender gap narrows.

That means the sheer numeric differences between male and females are not much different for blacks than for other ethnic groups. But other factors have conspired to frustrate and thwart black partnering, and many of them are steeped in America's long-running bad habits. For starters, black men continued to be charged, prosecuted, and locked up at disproportionate rates. At the end of 2005, there were 547,000 black men in jail or prison. Since there are only 16,465,000 black males in the entire country, that means that a sizeable number of black men are out of circulation (though certainly some inmates are married, and others would be despite their woeful circumstances). By comparison, there are 103,773,000 white males in the country, and only 459,700 of them were in jail or prison at the end of 2005. No one questions the correlation between the hyper-incarceration of black men and the decrease in black marriage. Incarceration strips hundreds of thousands of black men of the most basic qualification for matrimony: liberty.

There are other factors exacerbating the black gender gap, such as unemployment. At the same time black women are being celebrated for unprecedented rates of advancement in professional fields, black men seem permanently affixed to the bottom rung of the employment ladder. Black men make up a disproportionately high number of the unemployed—often double the rate for white men. In the black community as much as anywhere, employment is valued as both a generator of income and benefits as well as affirmation of ambition, talent, and intelligence. It is an important indicator of eligibility.

Income may not be a consideration for all pairings, but I think it's safe to say that it is in most. Although some women don't mind if their men make less money than they do, most expect an able-bodied man to pull his weight and help them attain and maintain a certain lifestyle in fair proportion to the woman's contribution.

Because so many black men have either no job or a menial one, the labor gap has produced a class gap. In 1997, Harvard sociologist Orlando Patterson calculated that there were about 772 middle-class black men for every 1,000 middle-class black women. In Atlanta, which is arguably the most upwardly mobile predominantly black major city in the U.S. and home to some of the most accomplished black men in the country, there are 16,000 more black women than black men.

In the first years of the new century, black male unemployment is still rampant. At the same time, the media is looking more kindly upon black women, who are being feted for unprecedented rates of educational, career, and economic advancement. In March 2003, *Newsweek* magazine featured the rise of black women on its cover. The collection of articles was bittersweet. While it chronicled the accomplishments of black American women, it also took note of the widening chasm between the sexes.

Take college, for example. According to the *Journal of Blacks in Higher Education,* black women students outnumber black male students by 3:2 and, in some cases, 4:1. Only 16.5 percent of black men have a college degree, compared to 31.7 percent of white men. Consequently, earning potential is lopsided. The wage gap scares some men off, and some women, too. Shortage or no shortage, some women won't give the time of day to a man who is unemployed or one who earns considerably less than they do.

Of course, an education gap is the mother of unemployment. For example, the Washington, D.C.–based Justice Policy Institute reported in 2003 that "African American men in their early 30s are nearly twice as likely to have prison records (22 percent) than bachelor's degrees (12 percent)." In 2004, the *New York Times* reported this dire finding from a new study by scholars at Columbia, Princeton, and Harvard: "In 1995, 16 percent of black men in their 20s who did not attend college were in jail or prison; by 2004, 21 percent were incarcerated. By their mid-30s, 6 in 10 black men who had dropped out of school had spent time in prison." Such reports point to terrific personal and public policy failures that have extensive repercussions. Not the least of these repercussions is the potential to jeopardize the black American family, particularly as more and more black women are going in the other direction.

It is well documented that the rate of college-educated men increasingly trails the rate of college-educated women. But at the postgraduate level, the gap yawns. Black women are five times more likely to pursue master's degrees than are black men. The collective effect is a disparity in earning power and opportunity that dramatically affects equality and self-esteem—two areas that can efficiently kill a relationship.

Of course, there is also the abnormally high homicide rate for black men. A black man between the ages of 25 and 44 is 12 times more likely to be slain than a white man in the same age group, according to a report by the National Center for Health Statistics.

And there is HIV/AIDS infection, a disease that preys upon black men and women with abandon. The majority of new infections with HIV occur among black people, even though we are a minority population. According to Centers for Disease Control estimates published at the end of 2005, nearly 140,000 black men were infected with HIV/AIDS—one out of every 85 black American men 18 and older. Many black men live their lives "on the down-low"—leading heterosexual public lives but also maintaining gay relationships or encounters. Compared to the white community at large at this point in time, the black community places more of a stigma on homosexuality, and gay black men often hide or deny their orientation accordingly. Many black men in prison participate in gay encounters—willingly and unwillingly—and this also raises their risk of infection.

Of course, there are also the "outside" couplings. While the vast majority of blacks marry other blacks, interracial marriages are steadily rising. The incidence of black man–white woman marriages is twice the rate of black woman–white man unions.

The great unknown, of course, is how many black men are unmarriageable because they dread, fear, or otherwise reject commitment. Movies and sitcoms have us laughing about this, but it is a sobering condition. Think of how many good—no, great—women you know that are still waiting to exhale. Think of how many of them are the type that would have been swooped up as soon as she came of age back in the day. Why so many men seem to find us unmarriageable is a mystery.

I have a theory. I call it the Beyonce Syndrome. I think some men believe that no matter how wonderful their woman is, there is a gorgeous, sexy, spry, talented, and wealthy vixen—a Beyonce—out there for them, just waiting to be discovered. Even some of the real slugs seem to believe this; maybe it's because of all those gangsta videos where transparent losers are drowning in yearning young honeys.

Whatever is afoot, the forecast for black matrimony is bleak, and a lot of single black women are coming to grips with the fact that Mr. Right may be the most endangered black male of all.

Dr. Beverly Guy-Sheftall, founding director of the Women's Research and Resource Center at Atlanta's Spelman College, says that there are really only about 5 black men for every 10 black women, once social conditions are factored in. Consequently, as Guy-Sheftall told the *Cleveland Plain Dealer* in a September 2000 interview, "There are large numbers of African American women who are … resigned in some sense to a life of being alone."

. . .

As part of my research for this book, I talked with 130 black women from all walks of life, all ages, and all parts of the country, with a special focus on unmarried women. The unmarried women all had diverse reasons for being single. Of the 125 single women I interviewed, only three were adamantly opposed to marriage, and one of those three had been previously married.

Twenty of the single women (about 16 percent) admitted that they were actively seeking husbands and wanted nothing less than the contract. Except for the three who repudiated marriage, I suspect that some of the remaining 84 percent of the unmarried interviewees were also really eager for husbands, but for whatever reason, they didn't want to acknowledge it.

There is a wonderful array of options available to single women these days that our mothers and grandmothers never had. We can indulge in careers, hobbies, friendships, travel, and self-improvement campaigns without having to explain ourselves. We can own our own homes and be admired, and not pitied, for living alone. As sociologist Elisabeth Sheff has remarked, "Single does not necessarily mean lonely."

However, not one of the women I interviewed said she would pass up a chance for a solid, satisfying, and monogamous relationship. How much time and effort she was willing to invest in finding one, though, varied from woman to woman. Some insisted that the relationship would have to find them, and not the other way around.

For sure, the mating game is just one aspect of a single black woman's life. But let's begin there.

· 1 ·

What's a Girl to Do?

OUR SITUATION EVOLVED SOMETHING LIKE THIS: A little girl grew up protected and provided for by her father, nurtured and advised by her mother, and held to certain standards by the community. She was wooed and courted by a boy who had grown up under a similar set of circumstances. The two young people fell in love and took their place in the line of succession by making a commitment, taking vows, and becoming a father and a mother to protect, provide for, nurture, and advise the next little girl.

Things changed. That little girl grew up protected, provided for, nurtured, and advised equally by a father and a mother. Societal strictures lessened and loosened, and the little girl was encouraged to focus on her career before starting a family. In the middle of her career development, she submitted to some man's wiles and fell in love. They moved in together, and after having a little girl of their own, they got married and then divorced.

Things changed again. Their little girl grew up with part-time parents, few rules, and little enforcement of what rules remained. Society only asked that she get a basic education and obey the law, and little else she could do would shock or offend. She was recognized as every bit as capable, sovereign, and intelligent as any man. Her career opportunities were wide open, and her sexuality was liberated.

Unfortunately, her male peers mistook these developments to mean that their ancient rituals of courtship and commitment were obsolete, and that their traditional roles as husbands and fathers are disposable. The immutable biological and hormonal dictates prevail, of course, and the men seduce, but they don't commit.

The next little girl will grow up with a single mother and a father he or she may or may not ever know.

Thus does the old paradigm die. Forget marriage. Not even monogamy, or even false promises of it, are required for sex or procreation. Today it's not at all unusual for the Wham Bam to take place without even so much as a Thank You, Ma'am.

Consequently, black women of all ages and economic levels, from all regions, and in all shapes and sizes, have been victimized by their own gender's successes. The men who would be their partners don't want to commit or don't know what it means to do so. This is not true of all men, of course, but it is true for far, far too many of them.

. . .

And just as I was sitting in front of my computer, hanging on to some worn thread of hope that somehow, men will come around and recognize what fabulous women they're passing up and the fulfillment they're missing, I got an instant message from one of those fabulous women. Camille, a 26-year-old graphic designer, looks 19 but is already weary of having her heart broken. She tells me that she has written off "settling down" for now. She's had too many false starts to believe in it anymore, she says.

As the following exchange reveals, I'm fresh out of convincing words of consolation and am forced to rely on bromides and clichés.

CAMILLE: I really think I will get married when I'm around your age or maybe in my 40s, because I think the men of my generation will be ready.
ME: Time will tell, honey.
CAMILLE: I think they will be interested in me because I won't look my age. A friend and I have agreed to forget the idea of marriage and try to deal with dating.
ME: One step at a time, for sure.

CAMILLE: Even though you've been divorced, you should still be happy that you grew up when you did. It's so bad out here, Deborah; you just wouldn't believe it. I don't want you to get mad at me for saying this, but I think if I do have kids—if I get lucky enough—I think I'll be doing it on my own. I think I won't have any choice, based on what I'm seeing.

ME: There simply are not enough young men who have fathers (or other men) in their lives. They don't know how to do the commitment thing because they've never seen it done!

CAMILLE: Very true. I would like to break the cycle, but if you want kids nowadays, you have to be prepared to do it alone, because men my age and even 10 years older than me are not sticking around to help. I really think I'm going to try "something new" and start dating other races.

ME: Don't knock it till you try it!

CAMILLE: I've had more white and Latino guys try to holla at me this past month than black men in my entire life.

ME: Let me tell you what I've always said: If you are lucky enough to find someone who treats you like a princess, makes you happy, wins your faith, and rings your bell, should you really ask, "Does this come in black?"

CAMILLE: I get tired of hearing black men say that black women are angry, but I'll be one of the first to admit that they're damn right. We have given them life, raised their children alone, bailed them out of rough situations and jail, stood by their side, provided for them, and loved them unconditionally. And they've shit on us, so hell yeah, we're mad. In fact, they need to come up with a new word for mad.

ME: I hear you, believe me! Let me tell you: Some of the old ones aren't any better. They are selfish, egotistical, think you just want their money (or they just want yours), expect you to be grateful that anyone is interested in you, and on top of everything else they still want to make time with the

young girls. You need to ask God to help you accept His
will. He'll hook you up somehow.

CAMILLE: He already has by getting me out of a bad situation
with a man. I don't have the nerve to ask him to help me
anymore.

ME: I'm glad to hear you say, "He already has," because it's so
true. God is good, despite our tribulations. He's there with
us, as He promised. And, as for continuing to go to Him,
don't feel that you have used up your blessings. He gives
and gives and gives. Getting you out of the bad situation
was certainly a blessing. But He has more in store! Ask
Him! He likes that!

CAMILLE: I love you, Deborah, but I am going to be doing it
alone.

ME: Stop being so negative. Give other men a chance! Some of
them deserve some good fortune too! And there really are
some superb brothers out there.

. . .

I wish I had better news for Camille, but, alas, the prognosis for the
traditional two-parent family is not encouraging. It's why more and
more women are devising a "Plan B" that secures the parenthood
experience, even if it means going it alone. The Black Adoption Place-
ment and Research Center, which is based in Oakland, California,
reports that 40 percent of its adoptive parents are single black women.
In an interview with the *Washington Post*, the agency's executive director, Gloria King, put it bluntly: "They're not going to let marriage
stand in the way of them connecting with a child." This reflects a
national trend; according to the U.S. Department of Health and Human Services, about a third of public adoptions are made by single
women, and more than half of those new single moms are black and
in the 30-to-50 age group.

Certainly, a mature, financially stable mother is perfectly capable
of making a great home for a parentless child. As most of us can

attest, the rewards of motherhood are so manifold and continuous that the worries and responsibilities, heavy as they are, tend to pale in comparison. Even so, the trend does not bode well for the survival of the traditional black family.

Finding a suitable man has always been a crapshoot that requires patience and inventiveness. The difference now is that there are no hard-and-fast rules of conduct and no solidly defined gender roles (which of course isn't a bad thing). Today, the mating game requires more creativity and flexibility. Admittedly, that may be a bit of a spin, but I'm trying to stay positive here, if you don't mind. What else is a girl to do?

· 2 ·

Shrinkers

I CAN HALFWAY UNDERSTAND why I'm at home alone again on yet another Friday night. Except for my high heels, I'm still in my work clothes and hunched over a carton of Chinese food with a big glass of caffeine-free Pepsi on the side, my cigarettes on standby, and "America's Funniest Home Videos" on the tube. I'm 50 years old and, after another long work week, I'm tired. In this condition, about all I have to offer a man is my word that I will try not to snore too loudly.

Evidently, I am rather typical—average, even, when it comes to women "of a certain age," the women of the Baby Boomer generation born between 1945 and 1965. In the book *The Boomers' Guide to Online Dating*, Judsen Culbreth reported that many single women who are 50 or older enjoy dating, travel, and work—and want to stay single. Culbreth identifies four main reasons:

- the normalization of unmarried womanhood (no more "old maid" or "spinster" stigma)
- a de-emphasis on material accumulation (a preference for simple things now that the gold rush of younger years is over)
- a focus on family (grown children and the grandchildren)
- the absence of a need for what could be called the "functionality" of a husband (having babies, helping pay the bills, fixing things, taking out the trash)

Sociologist Elisabeth Sheff points out that the single state has loads of benefits—no one to report or account to, no logistics to coordinate or schedules to synchronize, no expenses to share or expenditures to explain, no habits that have to broken for the sake of someone else's allergy or distaste, and so on. There are friends and family, professional associations, travel, and a whole world out there to cultivate and enjoy.

Although I may have been considered a sad sister back in my mother's day, I am very close to normal now. Besides, I've had my shot at happily ever after. I've been married and divorced three times. I've raised three great kids. I've had the big pretty wedding, the small, intimate one, and the just-the-two-of-us one. I've had a big pair of feet to keep mine warm, I've slept in a spoon, and I've had big arms to help carry the groceries. I shouldn't be greedy about it.

. . .

But Gigi? Gigi hasn't had a real relationship in 14 years. She's had plenty of nibbles since then, but Gigi has always been choosy—frankly, she can afford to be. Not many suitors meet her requirements: "great listener, smart, tall, self-deprecating sense of humor, cute, muscular ... and he has to be able to fix things."

As she's gotten older, she has become even more particular. Although she recognizes that compromise might be in order, Gigi hates the idea of "settling." She wants no part of any man who is unemployed, so-so in bed, uneducated, religiously obsessed, or being supported by his mother (although it might be all right if he is supporting his mother). She wants to be married again, but she says the prospects are "bleak as hell." So, she keeps herself busy with her job in politics, caring for an elderly parent, helping out her kids, fighting traffic and paying taxes, and, every blue moon, taking a few minutes to talk to an old friend stuck at home on a Friday night.

And, like Shrinkers everywhere, she waits for that fateful knock, that fortuitous run-in, that coincidental timing that puts her, at last, face-to-face with the Mate Who Was Meant to Be.

How can that be? What's a woman like Gigi doing by herself at the end of the work week, when most gorgeous, smart, and single people are supposed to be out flaunting the fact that they're gorgeous, smart, and single? Why is she watching lions mate on "National Geographic" instead of cuddling up with her own king of the jungle?

"Girl, is this pathetic or what?" I say to her on the phone one night.

"Pathetic," she says, laughing.

"I don't know why we're laughing; this is not funny," I reply.

"No, it's not funny, but you know something, Deb? This is my life now. This is what happens when you spend all of your time working because it's the only thing you've got going on. By Friday night, you're too tired to go out and mingle with people. You're too tired to be cute."

"But, Gigi," I say, "I can't believe how many women this is happening to. Most of the sisters I know are without."

"Me too. But what can you do?"

"I suppose it would actually help if we went somewhere."

"I know, right? My kids are always saying, 'You're not going to meet anyone at sitting at home, Mom.'"

"Yeah, mine used to say I was waiting for Mr. Right to come knocking on my door. 'He's not coming to the house,' they'd say."

"Deb, I don't have the energy for getting dolled up and driving somewhere, parking, strutting in, and trying to look nonchalant. I really don't like that kind of scene anyway."

"I hear you."

"And I don't want to find him when I'm looking for him anyway; you know what I mean, Deb? I want to be surprised and swept off my feet. Is that corny?"

"No, you're just a romantic. You want some romance in your life. Not just sex."

"Exactly. But instead, my tired ass is sitting at home watching lions get it on."

"And I'm watching babies staring at each other and gurgling on 'America's Funniest Home Videos.'

"This is pitiful."

"Ain't that the truth?"

. . .

Gigi and I are Shrinkers. We want a man, but we're not willing to put much effort into finding him. It's not that we expect God to just leave him on the doorstep one day. But there was a time in our lives that men were like kudzu, sprouting up all over the place. Back then, juggling men and deciding who goes and who stays—that was our dilemma. After so many years of that kind of feast, it's kind of hard to accept that those days are over, and new times have dawned: drought and slim pickings.

It's especially tough on older Shrinkers, who rarely catch the eye of a handsome, strapping, virile young man anymore. Even when we do, that marvelous blush is extinguished by the ridiculousness that sweeps over us. For the most part, we are past the fit-and-fine man stage. We've passed the moment, and that window has closed.

Most of the men who are of an appropriate age for us are either married or so out of shape that it would take a couple of fire logs under our bottoms to get any real heat going. Of course, that's assuming we still want some sexual adventure in a relationship ... which, to hear us talk, most of us do. The irony, of course, is that we aren't what we used to be either. But we're picky nonetheless.

That is not to say that every middle-aged woman is past her prime. There are some real beauties out there—inside and out. They don't have a problem attracting men, but if they're Shrinkers, they may as well be invisible. Hunkering down on the sofa with take-out and a corny TV show is no way to make a relationship happen.

. . .

That's why Michelle and I used to go out practically every Friday night—and many Saturday nights—for a couple of years. Naturally, we wore black. We never planned it. In all of the back-and-forth phone calls about our nights on the town, we never once discussed attire. It was just a coincidence that we were similarly dressed. Black is, after all, excellent camouflage for the middle-aged truth.

The Sweet Young Things, the Flat Bellies, the veteran Bar Flies, and the Serious Hoochies would have opted for something more daring than black pantsuits or skirts, but our purpose was not to call too much attention to ourselves because … well, because we wanted to be careful about what we were asking for. It had been ages since either of us had tested the nightlife as single women, and although we were accomplished mothers and career women, the club scene made us nervous—even in a club that catered to the over-the-hill crowd.

The first time we went, we were delighted to find the place overflowing with revelers by the time we arrived, just past 9 p.m. Many of them had been drinking and carousing since happy hour and had established positions at the bar or the tables that ringed the dance floor. I'm convinced that the reason we were asked to dance again and again that night, and the reason many men sent drinks to our table, was simply because we were fresh meat. Once we became familiar faces in the place, both the dance invitations and the drinks dried up. Nothing else accounts for it. We were still the same fun-loving duo—dating ninjas, dressed head-to-toe in black.

To be honest with you, it was just as well that the men stopped catering to us, because almost none of them had any potential, if you know what I mean. A lot were old enough to be our fathers, a few were young enough to be our sons, a good many obviously had wives "back at the house," and far, far too many of them couldn't participate in a decent conversation. There was also the batch of horny cats that tried to grope us on the dance floor or, on a couple occasions, flat-out proposed a hitch in the sack. Michelle was always cool and precise in putting such men in their place, but me? I usually caused a minor scene, cussing the fools out and making them wish they'd never let a hand slip below my waist.

One night, a familiar fellow sauntered over to our table and promptly informed us that the regulars at the bar considered us unapproachable and somewhat snobbish. "High society" was how he put it. As this man explained it, our tendency to turn down offers was behind this reputation—that, coupled with the fact that we almost never worked the room upon arrival, went straight to our table, and stayed there all night. I was disturbed by the rap at first, but I soon came to appreciate it (however ill-informed it was), since at least it meant we were not being seen as eager or desperate. Of course, we knew we weren't desperate, although one might wonder why we had nothing better to do with our Friday (and Saturday) nights.

Maybe location had something to do with it. There is hardly a worse place in the whole country to be black, female, and single than Washington, D.C. Women outnumber men substantially, and men who grew up in the nation's capital or who have spent a lot of years here tend to take advantage of the disparity. They know they're in demand—even the sorry ones. Maybe that's why Michelle and I never made a "love connection." We were too into the formalities—that slow-moving, let's-get-acquainted, I-want-romance-and-passion-and-conversation-and-laughs mode. We were being particular in a town where supply and demand were completely and perennially out of balance.

We kept hope alive for a long time, Michelle and I. But after a while, our partying attempts tapered off. Chinese food and Pepsi became my Friday night date. A glass of wine became Michelle's. Now, if I call her after 8:30 p.m., it's past her bedtime, and I talk to voicemail.

It's such a shame. What a woman Michelle is. For starters, she's unusually tall and striking. She's got a sharp mind, a winning personality, a pretty face, and obvious class. For good reason, her former husband had adored her, but some bad things happened toward the end of their 25th year together, and the marriage fizzled.

For the first year after her divorce, Michelle was fine being relationship-less, or so it seemed. She had her kids and her job to keep her busy. She also had the exploration and discovery of newfound singlehood, which can be as exciting as it is daring after a quarter of a century as someone's wife.

But I think our unattached states hit us both hard the night we went to a fancy formal benefit for a local Jack & Jill chapter. The group had rented a spacious country-club ballroom for the event—a fund-raising dinner, auction, and dance—and organizers had outdone themselves, filling the place with magnificent flowers, exquisite food, great liquor, fantastic dance music, and thousands of tiny lights that made the room look like a twinkling night sky.

About 200 people came. They were all coupled off—husbands and wives, boyfriends and girlfriends. If there was a single man in the whole bunch, we didn't see him. Well, okay, there was this one guy. Let me put it this way: You know how they say a tux can make any man look great? That's a lie.

As couple after couple took to the dance floor, Michelle and I sat by ourselves at a table, playing with our food, swirling our drinks, staring at folks undulating to music we loved, and trying our best not to look wistful, lonely, or envious, which of course we were.

On another occasion, Michelle invited me along on a trip to Nantucket, Massachusetts, a gorgeous, sunny island getaway whose inhabitants are, practically without exception, rich. She was there for three days of dinners and parties related to her work as a lobbyist, and she'd secured a lovely hotel room near the bay. When I flew in a day later, she was lazing in the tiny airport, looking like relaxation incarnate.

"You're going to be sick," she said. Although I knew where she was going with this, I quizzically arched an eyebrow, urging her on.

"It's beautiful, exquisite, private, peaceful, and luxurious here," she said. "The staff waits on you hand and foot. The food is good too. The booze is good. The parties are happening ..."

"... and here we are, two home girls, with no men to have a good time with," I added.

"You got it," she said.

"And don't expect to find it here either," she cautioned. "I've see two black men since I've been here. One was a busboy and the other looked like he was about 10. And everybody else is coupled off."

We had a good time anyway. We always do. But it sure would be nice to just once pick up the phone and say, "Guess what I'm doing tonight?" and have the answer be something other than sponge-painting the walls.

Eventually, Michelle started missing being in a relationship. She didn't want anything too fancy—just someone to talk to, go to the movies with, and take an occasional trip with. Someone other than me, of course.

I took no offense, of course, because I knew exactly where she was coming from. I'd been thinking the same thing. Although I love Michelle like a sister, there's a certain feeling I'm looking for that we can't provide for each other. We're both proud women, feminists, good providers for our families, and all that. We also want the right man in our lives. So, we try to keep hope alive, but the problem is that we aren't doing a damned thing to make it come alive.

"I have a man who's interested in me now, but he's married. And there's another one who's not married, but all he cares about his Porsche, his Armani suits and name-dropping all night long. I don't enjoy being out with him, so I don't go," Michelle explained.

Nor is she into younger men. "My sons are young men," she declared. "I can't see myself dating someone from their peer group. Lord, no. Meanwhile, the ones who are my age don't do anything for me. So, I'm just going to enjoy my work and enjoy my kids and do some traveling. This is just how it's going to be. If someone comes along, he's going to have to find me."

. . .

Now Charmaine? She really needs to check herself. She lives in the Los Angeles area, goes to school part-time, and substitute teaches. She is petite, smooth-faced, firm-bodied and young—a 30-year-old who looks 19 or 20. She wants to get married some day, but sees no prospects on the horizon.

Charmaine has motive and opportunity. Her phone constantly rings, and her e-mail inbox is full of invitations to parties, receptions, and galas. Charmaine rarely accepts them. In fact, she hardly ever goes out anywhere. When she's not teaching, she has her nose in a textbook or pointed at a computer screen. For leisure, she works out or drives down to the beach for long, solitary walks. She turns down most of the invitations because, according to her, most of them are usually just glorified booty calls.

"I don't know," says Charmaine. "I always feel like I'm on display, like a prized heifer waiting for some guy to bid on me. It's so obvious that people are trying to find a hook-up, and I can't stand being mistaken for one of those people."

"But isn't it possible that someone nice, compatible, and interesting could be standing around the punch bowl?"

"Yeah, but I wouldn't talk to him because I would assume he's one of 'them'."

"Maybe you're reading too much into it," I say.

"Maybe, but I doubt it. I mean, it's not like I haven't given it a try. What I've seen tells me my theory is right. They're all looking, and they're all so fake and shallow. If they're not, they're afraid to settle down because they think something better might be out there. Or they really want a white girl or a Latina girl. Or they don't want to stop hanging out with their boys. Or their mama doesn't like you. It's always something. So, I stopped believing it's going to happen when I'm looking. I think it's going to catch me off-guard."

"You think he is going to appear?"

"I do."

"When you're on the beach by yourself?"

"Maybe."

"You think he's just going to come strolling up on the beach, rising up out of the surf, huh?"

"I just believe in fate, and if it's meant to be, yes, he could rise up out of the surf."

See what I mean? That's what true Shrinkers believe. They don't see that they have to make any real effort at finding a mate, because fate will take care of it for them. Mr. Right will fall through the ceiling tiles or something, or bump your fender in the grocery store parking lot. At least Gigi and Michelle and I have something of an excuse—we've been around the block a few times, and we're tired.

But Charmaine? At 30, she's just hitting her stride and she's already over it.

. . .

Linda, a sales representative from Orlando, is 10 years older than Charmaine, but you know that 40 is nothing like it used to be—they say it's the "new 30." Even with a decade on Charmaine, she's hung up her high heels too soon. Linda is practically invisible on the dating circuit. She spends most of her free time involved in church work or trying out new sushi bars with her girlfriends. Although there are a lot of men in her church, Linda says most of them are married or too old. And sushi bars are hardly known for their black male clientele. Like most Shrinkers, Linda can't explain why she's not doing more to bring her wish for a mate to fruition. "Maybe," she wonders, "we're just lazy."

. . .

She'd known that marrying a guy she had only known for three months—and on the rebound, too—probably wasn't going to work. When she met her husband-to-be, she had just gotten out of a long, difficult relationship with a mercurial character, a Jekyll-and-Hyde type whose two-faced routine got to be too much. Angie had known better, but she did it anyway.

The marriage was nearly four years old when Angie, pregnant with the couple's daughter, decided to leave her husband. He attended the birth, but Angie knew there wouldn't be a family—there was too much water under the bridge.

It was a struggle at first. Angie had two daughters—the eldest was from a previous relationship—and a burning need to start over. The threesome moved to Atlanta, where Angie quickly found work.

"I met this guy my first day on the job," she recalls. "He worked in the shipping department. He told me I looked uptight, like I needed a massage. You know what? I let him massage my back. Then he gave me his pager number—not his phone number, mind you—his *pager number*. Look out."

"Was there anything to the pager warning?" I ask.

"Oh, he finally gave me his number. But, listen to this: I called him one day and a woman answered. He told me that she was his cousin. I'm thinking, 'Your cousin?' Of course, it was actually his wife. He had gone out to gas up his wife's car and get milk for the baby."

"The baby? He had a baby too?"

"The baby! That was too much. I confronted him about it, of course. I said, 'When we first started talking, I asked you, 'Are you married?' There wasn't anything ambiguous about it—are you married?' And he swore up and down that he wasn't. So, that was the end of that. But we dated for two and a half years. Can you believe that?"

When Angie and her girls moved back to Maryland, she went to work for a television production company. Eventually, she was promoted to business manager. Her social life hasn't matched her career success, but she did have one promising relationship.

"He was the band director at my daughter's school," says Angie. "I'm pretty tall, you know, and he's shorter than me, but that didn't bother me. He's a cute man. We dated for a year, but it was awkward for my daughter and for him. Eventually, we broke it off."

Now that she's 40 and facing the prospect of an empty nest in the next few years, Angie is looking for the opportunity to meet a "nice" man. Shrinker that she is, though, she's most likely to head for home at the end of the day instead of venturing out where eligible men gather. Bars are not her thing, she says, and in other venues, the men are already taken.

"Don't ask me what I'm waiting for," she says. "I know I need to get out there."

. . .

Gigi, Charmaine, Linda, and Angie all need to get back out there. The male population is being deprived by their decisions to stay home and knit fantasies about Mr. Right. Those faces, that hair, those figures, those personalities, those good hearts, and those quick minds—it's all such a waste.

Some Shrinkers are more hopeful than others. Some aren't sure the whole fantasy about relationships is a total waste of time. Not all are as jaded as Michelle and I. We like to say that all we attract anymore are the four Ms: monsters, morons, midgets, and misers (there's a fifth, too, actually: marrieds). It's not a joke or an exaggeration. If I'm not getting hit on by someone young enough to be my son or old enough to be my father, I'm getting hit on by someone even more unappealing.

Once, I was in a doughnut shop and briefly met eyes with an ugly, squat little gnome of a man sipping a cup of hot chocolate. I nodded, he nodded, and I quickly grabbed my goodies and left.

As I backed out of my parking space, the little man knocked on my window. "Excuse me," he said, "do you know where I can get a lottery ticket around here?"

Political creature that I am, I almost gave the man my spiel about the evils of lotteries—how they take advantage of poor people, how they ultimately end up robbing state treasuries, and how he would be better off investing in doughnut holes. But I thought better of that and simply told him, "No. Sorry."

Those two words had barely cleared the air when he said, "Are you married?"

"Why do you ask?" I said.

"Because I'd like to call you sometime and take you out."

Lord, have mercy.

I described the whole sorry episode to Michelle. When she finished laughing, she said, "I told you, we might as well give up. Our time is over. All that's out there for us are the four Ms."

Actually, we're neither as heartless nor as hopeless as our quip implies. We're also not as amused as our laughter suggests. It's good for a laugh, but 'tain't funny, my friends.

Swingles

IN THE SISTERHOOD OF SINGLE BLACK WOMEN, the Swingle is the polar opposite of the retiring, hesitant, and often pessimistic Knitter. She doesn't identify with the plight of single sisters who can't seem to connect, and she can't commiserate with women who are frustrated by the dearth of available men. If you're having a pity party, she's a party pooper. If it's a Waiting to Exhale gathering, she's breathing easy. She is the swinging single—the Swingle.

Swingles come in two versions. One is not discriminating—or at least not very discriminating—about the men she sees. Those standards vary from woman to woman, but their variety accounts for some peculiar, and even sometimes preposterous, couplings. Sometimes even married men make the cut. The other kind of Swingle only chooses men who are generally considered to be desirable—the ones who are already in high demand.

Either version is a threat to the rest of us. They're successful in the marketplace, and they're often hoarders. Who can blame them?

· · ·

Monique, a 33-year-old journalist, lives in a nice house in a nice neighborhood in a nice slice of northern Virginia, just outside the nation's capital. Her home, which she shares with a Yorkshire terrier named Sheba, is tidy and well appointed, but there's a lot Monique wants to do to the house. The living room is too long for her taste, for example, the kitchen is too small, and the backyard needs landscaping.

But the master bedroom, which not even Sheba can enter, is luxurious, exotic, and breathtaking. Tables and windowsills are laden with candles and incense burners. The soft shades over the windows are remote-controlled. A gauzy bronze canopy wafts over the gigantic California-king bed. The walls are sepia. Huge plump pillows encircle a low round table in a sitting area near a large screen TV and sophisticated CD player. "That's where all my money has gone," she says, as if she needs to. "It's my retreat, my spa, and my pleasure temple. My special place."

Monique swears that not many men get to see her special place, but that's not due to lack of interest. This woman always … always … has a man waiting at her side or in the wings. Woman after woman will show up at affairs alone, with coworkers, or with women friends, but Monique invariably sashays in with an escort.

"Where do you get these men?" I ask.

"Different places," she says. "I met one at a grocery store; I've met guys at the bookstore, in the mall, at church, at the Kennedy Center, in bars, and on the subway."

"Okay, I get it."

"They're out there."

"Then why do you think so many women are having trouble making a connection?" I wonder.

"I really can't say. Maybe they're too serious."

"What do you mean?"

"You know how we say men are dogs? I think that's true, but I don't mean it in a negative way."

"Oh, there's a good way to be a dog?"

"Naw, girl. What I'm talking about is … you know how they say dogs can smell fear? Well, I think men can sniff out desperation in women."

"But, Monique, you don't think that every woman who is alone is desperate, do you?"

"No, no. That's not what I'm saying. Okay, desperate may be the wrong word. What I'm trying to say is that a lot of women are looking for men, and I think men pick up on that."

"So what if they're looking?"

Exasperated, Monique lets out a big sigh. "I just think that if you go somewhere with the idea that you're trying to find a man, instead of going to see the movie, or have a drink, or whatever, then men can sense that, and it scares them off. Some of them."

"But you know as well as I do that a lot of them are out there looking for women."

"That's true. But don't you think they're upfront about it? They don't really pretend that they're not looking."

According to Monique's theory, women like to appear nonchalant about meeting men—not indifferent, necessarily, just cool. Like Michelle and me at the bar. But she thinks men can tell that a woman is faking disinterest and that she is really scanning the joint for prospects. "What they can't tell," says Monique, "is what they're seeking a man for: Do they want a sex partner, a companion, a provider, or a husband?"

I find myself frustrated by Monique's theory. "Of course they can't tell that. So what?"

"Well, if they can't tell, some men are anxious about approaching a new woman," Monique replies. "They think she might be a 'fatal attraction' or something."

"Oh, that's ridiculous."

"Why is it ridiculous? Some women are clingy and possessive."

"And some are not."

"Right, but if the guy thinks that she came there just to find a man, there's a chance that she is."

"And, according to your theory, that scares him off and keeps him from even approaching her."

"Correct."

"Then how are women supposed to attract new men? What's your secret?"

"I don't care whether I meet them or not. I really don't."

"And they can sense that."

"They can sense that, and it turns them on, I think."

"But maybe the reason you don't care is because you have so many men already, and you don't need any more."

Monique snickers at this. She can't deny it. She's a player. "But how did I get all these men?" she asks, setting me up. "I got them by not looking for them."

"So your advice to women is?"

"Go to the movie to see the movie. Go to the bar to dance and have a good time. Go to church to hear the sermon or the choir. Pretend that there will be no men there, and don't expect to meet anybody."

This is getting complicated. "But, Monique, you can't necessarily help thinking you could meet someone wherever it is you're going."

"I know that."

"So, what's the alternative, then? Act like you're not looking? You just said that a man can sniff out pretense and phoniness."

Monique won't look me in the eye. She shuffles the food around on her plate, pokes a forkful into her mouth, and chews a bit before speaking again.

"All I know is that you have to train yourself not to look for men. Let them find you."

That's easy for a Swingle like Monique to say. Men are always "finding" her. The famous shortage that leaves so many black women single doesn't seem to have affected her in the least. Maybe attitude is key. Maybe it does ooze through. Maybe there is a fear factor in men that gives them some kind of extrasensory perception when it comes to women on the make.

But then I considered Monique's bedroom, and how elaborately and sensuously decorated it is. It's decorated for a love connection, in my opinion. That doesn't seem to fit with someone who is blasé about love, does it?

I ask Monique about this paradox.

"Girl, you're reading it the wrong way," she protests. "I fixed up that bedroom to make me feel sensual and pampered and comfortable. You notice all of the candles have been lit. That's not because I had a lover there recently. It's because I treat myself to candles and incense and music, just like I do to long, hot baths and massages. What I'm trying to get over to you is that I believe in loving yourself, and being good to yourself."

"And when you step out …"

"You're cool, because you're not looking for someone to make you feel special. You're already special."

I'm nodding. Now I get it. If you build your own self-esteem, they will come. That's what Monique is trying to say. It's a good theory, but not a perfect one. I know too many women who are extremely self-confident—and still alone.

A mutual friend thinks that Monique is just one of those women who can't miss with men. "She's one of those women that men just like," says Desiree. "They're just attracted to her. I don't know … it's pheromones or something. They've just got that thing that men like. You know that movie, *Something About Mary*? It's like that. All different kinds of men just fall all over Monique. That girl's got men to spare."

"Maybe we ought to get a bunch of women together and go over there and whip her ass," I joke.

"And then all those men would be at the hospital, bringing her flowers," Desiree wisecracks.

"Girl, hush."

"You know it's the truth. She's just got it like that."

. . .

Monique's philosophy had a familiar ring to it. It's what we've been told most of our lives—you have to first love yourself before you're ripe for loving, and being loved by, someone else. It's what Claudette Sims counseled in her book, *Loving Me: A Sisterfriend's Guide to Being Single and Happy*. Sims wrote, "We must stop saving up all our love for the Maybe Man and start spending some of that on ourselves, filling our own hearts and souls with joy and happiness and peace. We must learn to fall in love with ourselves, so if we never meet that special person with whom we thought we'd spend the rest of our lives, we still feel loved."

Maybe that's what Monique meant. Maybe that's why her bedroom is so plush. It's designed to accommodate her most welcome and important lover: herself.

. . .

There's something about Patrice too. She's just past 50 years old, has been married and divorced twice, and has two sons—one in his 20s and the other a teenager. Patrice is a lobbyist with a spectacular condo on the Chesapeake Bay. Right now, she's in an exclusive relationship that seems to be going great. If it falters, though, not to worry—Patrice has men out the wazoo. Even her ex-husbands are crazy about her.

Some, she insists, are just friends. Others have been "Good Time Charlies"—men with plenty of money, or ones who were willing to spend what they had on Patrice. One was just a ... what shall we call him? ... a "serviceman." Without any pretense of romance or commitment—in fact, with a mutual understanding that romance and commitment were no-nos—he shared Patrice's bed, sometimes stayed over for breakfast, and then would be promptly dispatched, with no strings, no expectations, no demands, and no guilt tripping. It gives a whole new meaning to the term "safe sex."

Patrice says she knows when she really cares about a man because she cares if he votes.

"What?" I ask, confused by the peculiar litmus test.

"If he matters to me, I want him to be responsible and upstanding and to take care of his rights. I want to see him do well. If he's just a fuck buddy, the sex is good, and you don't care if he votes."

Unlike Monique, Patrice doesn't have a theory about why it rains men for some women while others suffer through the drought. All she knows is that she's never thirsty.

. . .

Ten friends, all single black women, gathered over pasta and wine to talk about the men in their lives (or lack thereof). Michelle and I were among them. Half were divorced. Half had never been married. The youngest was 40, and the oldest was 54.

Lynne, one of the never-marrieds, looked a good 10 years younger than her 44 years. "I came close to marriage twice. In one case, when he did propose, it was out of desperation. I was moving to Washington, and he thought he was going to lose me. I didn't want to marry someone in that situation. When I told him I was going anyway, he tried to possess me. He said, 'You don't even know anybody.' I said, 'I know me.' That blew his mind."

Most of Lynne's closest friends were also single. They didn't bug her about not being married, but other intimates did. "My mother never comes out and says it, but I know, deep in her heart, now that I'm getting older, she's wishing I would find someone. Even though she knows how secure working for the federal government can be, she still says, 'Keep your antennae up.' She also worries that I'm too set in my ways."

At one point, Lynne dated a 30-year-old attorney. "His sexuality was bold, so I had to step on up to the plate. I've got my little thong on and all," she said. "But he was too adventurous. He wanted a *ménage à trois,* and I just couldn't handle that. But I was in a drought, so I stuck with him anyway even though the relationship was pretty much reduced to drive-by booty calls. The sex was great, but I felt terrible afterward. Eventually I cut that loose."

Lynne was so pretty and personable that it was hard to imagine her having a rough go of it in the dating department. She kept the faith, though.

"For the past four months, every Friday night, I put myself out there," said Lynne. "I go to a different hotel bar or two every Friday to test the atmosphere. I've been there alone, and I've been there with friends. I always dress for the occasion, just in case."

"Any luck?" someone asked.

"Well, the men are there, that's for sure," Lynne said. "They're generally in the 28-to-40 range. They're all different ethnicities; they're alone and in groups. When there are couples, it's mostly black men with white women, which is hurtful."

"But have you had any luck in those places?" I asked.

"I haven't exchanged numbers with anyone yet," she said. "I've had some good conversations, but when they find out you're in your 40s and have never been married, I think that sets them back. They think, 'There's something wrong with this chick.' Some will actually say, 'Oh, you must be hard to please.'"

Patrice piped up. "If I meet a guy in his 40s who hasn't been married, I'll admit that I wonder if something's wrong."

Another woman, Jeannette, jumped in. "Maybe they think there's nothing they can do for you."

"They have all kinds of ideas about women my age not being married, apparently," says Lynne. "So some of my girlfriends and I have started telling them we're divorced."

"You're kidding," says Michelle.

"No, I'm not," Lynne replies. "It's sad, but that seems to be okay. They're not afraid of a divorced woman, but a woman in her 40s who has never been married? They treat me like I'm some kind of freak."

. . .

Throughout the conversation, Maggie, 43, sat on the sofa, taking it all in and saying nothing. She was more put-together than the rest of us: Some were in jeans or other casual clothing, but Maggie was wearing a cinnamon-colored suit. Her jewelry glistened. Her nails were perfectly done. Her auburn hair looked neat and freshly styled.

Maggie came from a large, close-knit family. She almost married her first love when she was 17 and he was 19. But he joined the army, and when Maggie talked about joining him, her family objected. "So we kept writing each other and setting goals together," she said. "But over time, he failed to meet any of those goals, and that was that."

She almost married again in the 1980s, in her 20s, but she decided she wasn't ready. So she got comfortable with the single life.

"I'm still searching for that significant other," she said. "I know that it will happen. I've been praying over it. My family puts a lot of pressure on me—especially my brothers-in-law. I'll get married if someone rocks my boat. He has to be understanding."

. . .

As Lynne explained her frustration on the dating scene, Maggie quietly sipped her drink and smiled occasionally as the rest of us guffawed. When Lynne finished recounting her escapades, Maggie cleared her throat.

"You have to know where to find men," said Maggie. "It's the Prime Rib for lunch on Fridays, and the 701 on Friday nights. The Caucus Room is also good. On weekends in the fall, there's a sports bar downtown that's great during the day when the games are on. The Cobalt Room at the Ritz-Carlton is another place. And the library, over at the Regis? It's good on Thursdays and Fridays."

The room fell silent.

"Wow," someone said. "You've really got it down."

"You just have to know where to find quality men," Maggie said. "You can find them at quality places, and each place has its day. Oh, the Sequoia is good for happy hour."

As soon as she said that, her cell phone rang. It was the second call she'd taken since the evening had begun, and both were from men she was dating.

As the rest of us rehashed old relationships and laughed at ourselves, Maggie gathered her purse and jacket and told us that she wouldn't be joining us at the nightclub later that evening. Maggie had a date.

She fluffed her hair, kissed the hostess goodbye, and was gone. A puff of envy blew across the room, but no one acknowledged it. Instead, we plunged into the cheesecake and champagne—as if we were the ones with something to celebrate.

. . .

There is probably no group of black women that enjoys the single life like the young ones—the ones with the flat stomachs and firm, smooth skin who belt their pants at the hips … low on the hips. These are the ones who may indulge their inner party girl without the burden of time pressures, for time is on their side. There's plenty of time left for finding "the one." For now, they can relax and just be Swingles extraordinaire.

When Camille of Dallas or Alexis of Cleveland or Stephanie of Los Angeles or Marguerite of Miami enter a room, the rest of the women watch their odds of meeting a man drop like a stone. Each is to the modern social scene what Clara Bow was to 1920s Hollywood—the "It Girl." Men of all ages sway a little when one of these women passes by.

"My friends always say I'm so lucky because I never had a problem attracting men," says Marguerite, a stunning woman with high cheekbones and almond-shaped eyes. "So I see a lot of guys. Sometimes it's just kind of a mini-date, like walking through South Beach, or shooting a couple of games of pool. Sometimes, it's the full Monty—going out to dinner and then going to a club. But yeah, I stay pretty booked up."

Camille, 23, has narrowed her field to three. None of them lives in Dallas, and she likes it that way. "I'm not interested in a serious relationship right now," she says. "I fell in love for the first time at the age of 18, and I've looked forward to being married since then. I cannot wait to be a wife and mother. But it has to be with the right man … not just any man. I hate to admit it, because I love black men more than anything in this world, but they seem to have a hard time settling down. They're usually afraid of marriage, and they say that we sistahs have bad attitudes. I think time will help with some of that. I'm just waiting for men my age to grow up, I guess."

Alexis dates with a vengeance. There are six men in her life right now. Four of them know she's seeing other men, but two think they've got her to themselves.

"How do you pull that off?" I ask.

"They have to mind their own business!" she says. "I don't tell them everywhere I'm going, and I don't let them think they control me. If I am going out with Trey and Christian calls, I just tell Christian I have too much studying to do—he knows that when I'm studying, I don't want to be bothered—and that's it."

"Why don't you just tell them that you're seeing other men?" I ask. "You're free, single, and young. You don't have to lie to them."

"It's not like that," Alexis protests. "It's not like I have to lie to them."

"But you are lying to them."

"It's not really a lie. It doesn't hurt anybody."

"Alexis, it's a lie. It's deception."

"But, see, if I told them, they couldn't handle it. It would be over. Christian would probably freak out and do something stupid to himself."

"Good grief. Then why do you even want men like that?"

"'Cause they're cool. They're fun to be with. I like them."

"Fine, but you have to be fair to them."

"I am being fair."

"How is it fair to them to let them believe they have a monogamous relationship with you when they don't?"

"How do I know they don't have other girls?"

"Do you think they might?"

"They could. I don't think so, but they could."

"Don't you think you have the right to know?"

"Not really. It's not like I'm having sex with a bunch of men, so I'm not putting them in danger. We aren't married, so I don't really owe them anything, I don't think, as long as I treat them right."

"Okay, Alexis."

"I'm for real. I'm just having a good time. I'm 22 years old. Twenty-two. I'm not thinking about settling down. I'm trying to get my degree and do something with my life. This is just passing the time until I get things together."

"And then you're going to tell the guys what's up, or cut them loose, or settle down with one of them?"

"Maybe."

"Alexis."

"Okay, yes. But until then I'm not trying to make a commitment. There are too many men out here to have fun with."

Arf.

. . .

As a part-time student and a part-time hostess at one of L.A.'s hottest spots, Stephanie sees a parade of men: beautiful-people kind of men, as well as the garden variety. With brown hair in long African twists, a model's body, a quick mind, and a ready smile, she fits the scene. In fact, she gets asked out so much that she occasionally puts herself on a "man fast."

"I'm not complaining, you understand, but I get exhausted from dating too much," she says. "Listening, talking, and paying attention takes a lot of energy. The men I date are really nice guys, and I like to treat them well, but it takes a lot of work to be on top of the game, so to speak. So, I take a couple of weeks' hiatus about every other month. To recharge."

I ask Stephanie if all the men are equally "nice."

"Pretty much," she says. "They're all different, but they're all really interesting. One is an architect, one is an actor, one is a graduate student, one is a banker ..."

"How many are there?"

"I'm not sure. They're in rotation, so it's hard to keep count." Stephanie says, flashing a wide pearly grin.

"Nothing serious with any of them?"

"Hmmmm. Serious." Stephanie taps her teeth with a straw. "No, I wouldn't say any of them were really serious. Some are more serious than others, but nothing like engagement or anything."

"You're just not a one-man kind of woman."

"I wouldn't say that. I could be. But a man has to earn that, and so far no one has."

"So, in the meantime ..."

"In the meantime, I'm just enjoying the company of a lot of very nice men. And not to sound vain or anything, but I think they're enjoying my company too."

. . .

"I have a rule," says Cassandra. "I only date one man at a time. But I always date someone."

Forty-nine and twice-divorced, Cassandra is a Swingle by necessity. "I just don't feel right going out by myself, and I'm too old to go out with a bunch of women," she says. "Plus, when you go out with other women, it kills your action. It intimidates men, because they think you're all desperate, or horny, or man-bashing."

This is not happy news for those of us who go out alone or with their women friends, and I tell her so. Cassandra didn't back down.

"You need to break that habit, Deb," she says. "You just need one man to be your escort for receptions or dinners."

"But I don't go out much," I reply.

"Well, you need to change that too. I'm surprised to hear that. You don't seem like the homebody type."

"No, I'm a Shrinker."

"A Shrinker? What's a Shrinker?"

"That's what I call single women who would like to have a relationship but don't do much of anything to make that happen. Instead, they just sit at home, whiling away the time."

"Oh, I get it. Well, you don't impress me as a Shrinker."

"But I am."

"Then you need to change that."

"But, Cassandra," I say, "You just said I shouldn't go out alone or with my girlfriends, so how am I supposed to change it?"

"Call somebody."

"Call somebody? Who am I supposed to call?"

"You know some men. It doesn't have to mean anything. Just call one of the men you know and invite him to go out with you somewhere—somewhere where people will see you."

"And why won't that kill my action?"

"It might for that night, but it will establish you as a dating woman, honey. The next time you're out, people will know you are available."

It didn't make sense to me. If Cassandra's theory held up, wouldn't showing up with a man lead people to think I was unavailable? If I went out after that faux date without him, wouldn't that be breaking her never-go-out-alone rule?

"No, see, here's how it works. You go out and are seen with a man. Then you go out again with another man. And then another. That shows everyone that you're a dating woman, but not in a committed relationship, see? I'm telling you, it works."

Cassandra, who lives in Chicago, is a marketing executive. Gimmicks, image-making, and strategy are her business. Don't you know she's good at what she does?

. . .

Lorraine, who's in her 50s, just got out of a 10-year relationship. That's been her habit. She dates one man at a time for long stretches—"10, 12 years, usually," she says. Each time she's had these relationships, people have expected them to get married—including the men themselves. Lorraine was tempted a couple of times, but she says, "I don't know if I really would have gone through with it."

She grew up in a large family with four other siblings. All of her brothers and sisters are married, and all, says Lorraine, "have issues."

"Our father was very controlling, and that stayed in the back of my mind as something I didn't want for myself," says Lorraine. "I like my independence. I travel a lot, get massages, take care of myself, and do what I want to do. I like men, but I don't think I'm the marrying kind. If I were, my ideal life would be to be married maybe two days a week."

Now that's she's unattached again, Lorraine gets a lot of questions from friends and family about the whereabouts of the dearly departed, but they give her no pressure to replace him or jump the broom. "I've always been so independent. They wouldn't dare pressure me," she says.

Nor does she feel any pressure from anywhere else. "Society doesn't program us this way," Lorraine notes. "Society suggests you're supposed to get married and have children. But look at the divorce statistics, and you can see that something's not working right. All I can say is that I thank God for Oprah, because she doesn't make us feel like we have to follow the programming."

· 4 ·

Tickers

THE TICKERS know all about the calendar and the clock. They're the ones who think time is running out on their dreams of romance and, in some cases, of marriage and children. All the talk about the shortage of men is nothing new to them; they've been dealing with the deficit for years. But awareness of time is not the same as desperation or neurosis. The Tickers I talked to are accomplished and steady. The absence of a man has not been a handicap or a hindrance for them, but it is at odds with what they had envisioned for themselves. They have not given up on the idea, but they do have a "point of no return" in mind—a hash mark beyond which, they say, they will no longer consider the notion of marriage.

· · ·

Valerie pulls the Tootsie Roll Pop out of her mouth with a smack and waves it at me. "If things aren't looking better by the time I'm 40, four years from now, I'm going to find a man with good genes and get pregnant," she says. "I would prefer to have a great man at my side, but if I have to do it alone, I will. I'm going to be a mother."

Valerie is as no-nonsense as they come. She is famously frank, but witty too, and the combination has a softening effect on her tough talk. If she says she's going to have a child, man or no man, it wouldn't be a waste of money to buy a shower gift right away.

She was married for nearly three years, but she and Gerard fought so much that she was afraid she would hate her husband before long. "I already resented him, and I didn't want to hate him," she says. "I'm fairly sure he was feeling the same way. So we just put that one to bed." She hasn't had much luck in the dating arena since then.

"You know, I'm not every man's cup of tea," she says, waving that candy again. "A lot of men can't take a woman who just puts it all out there like I do. It's the same way with work. Fortunately, my boss likes my style. He knows he can trust me, and that I'm going to tell him what's good for him. That's why I'm a good administrative assistant. I don't kiss up. I'm respectful, but I don't kiss up."

"But in other relationships, that's problematic?"

"Yes, it is."

"But some men like women like you."

"That's what I keep hearing. I just can't seem to find any of them."

"How much do you want a man in your life, Valerie?"

"Not enough to change who I am!"

"That's not what I'm saying. I'm only trying to determine whether or not you are a Ticker … if you've got a timetable in mind for finding a man. Whether it's at the front of your brain or not."

"Oh, it's at the front of the brain all right. I am a normal woman, you know. I want love and happiness like anybody else. But the only thing I've got a timetable for is having children. I want to have children—at least one—by the time I'm 40."

"What's magic about 40?"

"Nothing's magic about it. It's just my cutoff. I don't want to be too old with my children. My plan was to have a first child with Gerard after we had been married about four years. Since we barely made it to three years, that didn't happen. But I'm still hoping to find someone I can love and who loves me. But if I don't by four years from now, I'm getting pregnant."

Valerie's plan is more than a notion. She already has three men in mind as potential fathers of her yet-to-be conceived children.

"What's the plan?" I ask. "Are you going to develop a relationship with them or just come onto them?"

"Develop a relationship, hopefully."

"Then what are you waiting for, if the men are attractive to you now?"

"It's not that they're attractive to me in terms of having a relationship; they're attractive to me as fathers, because they are smart, healthy, and fine."

"So any future relationship would just be a fake?"

"No, I'd tell them what I'm going to do, but I would say we need to get to know each other first. We would have to be friends before and after."

Although Valerie isn't asking for my advice, I volunteer it nonetheless. I tell her to think and pray over her plan, because there's more at stake than just her happiness.

Think about the child too, I tell her. And be careful about "no-fault" pregnancies. That can open a whole other can of worms.

"Okay," she says. "I'll remember all that. And I'm praying over it now."

She takes another long drag on the Tootsie Roll Pop.

"But I'm having my baby."

. . .

Sinsi doesn't want to get married, and she isn't looking for a man to make a baby. She just wants someone to be around when her sons reach their teenage years.

"Not just for that," she says. "I want companionship and good sex and all that too. But I'm kind of in a rush for my boys, actually."

Sinsi's sons are 11 and 8. Their father, Sinsi's ex-husband, is out of the picture. He doesn't call, doesn't visit, and doesn't write. As the sister of three fatherless boys, she knows first-hand the struggle boys face without a man in their lives. They struggle to find men to bond with, and that often leads to the wrong kind of bonding—the gang kind, or the drug-peddling kind. The kinds that other fearless boys have shaped for themselves.

Sinsi is convinced that Joshua and Caleb will need a strong male presence in their lives to keep them on the straight and narrow. "I'm terrified of raising my boys alone," Sinsi says. "My brothers are really good to them, but they're in Cincinnati, and I can't leave New Orleans because of my job." So when she considers a relationship with a man, she considers it to be a four-way relationship.

"I feel like I'm under a lot of pressure to do this right for all of us," she says. "If I choose the wrong man for me, then I'll be a basket case. But if I choose the wrong man for them, the whole thing could backfire. So, you want to talk about picky? Honey, I'm picky."

It doesn't help that Sinsi is a social worker, because the job brings her face-to-face with her fears. Day after day, she counsels, tracks down, scolds, consoles, and assists young mothers whose sons have gone astray. According to Sinsi, the shortage of black men in the lives of black women has implications beyond the future of black love.

"Let me read you this," says Sinsi, shuffling papers. "'It was concluded that African-American adolescent boys with unmarried parents are at greater risk for developing low self-esteem compared with other African-American adolescents, but a more controlled and structure environment may buffer the effects of having unmarried parents.'"

"What's that from?" I ask.

"From the *Journal of Family Psychology*, September 2000. The article is by two psychologists from the University of California at Riverside."

"You got that from work?"

"I read the article when it was first published, but I've kept it close ever since," says Sinsi. "I use it in workshops a lot. I'm not going to read you the whole thing, but you have to hear this part: 'The African-American father's value in the home to his adolescent sons should not continue to be discounted.' See? That's a heads-up. That's like an assignment."

"So, if it weren't for your sons …"

"I could relax, right."

"But, Sinsi, come on now. You're a sharp, devoted mother to those boys."

"Thank you for that, but you heard what those psychologists said. They didn't say a good mother is of no use, but they said black boys need a father or at least a father figure."

"Well, okay, then. How's it going?"

"Pretty good lately. I just met a man about three weeks ago who, so far, seems to be the right one."

"How so?"

"Well, he's really calm and clean. He's well mannered. He knows a lot about sports, which the boys like. And he's real sexy toward me in a kind of subtle way. You know, he sneaks a look at me when the boys aren't looking and licks his lips."

"Uh-huh."

"He just seems really nice. I met him at a book signing."

"Oh, so he's a reading brother?"

"Oh, yeah. He reads a lot. He's very intelligent and a really good conversationalist. The only problem is that he goes for these spells without seeing me—not long, just two or three days—but I don't hear from him at all during that time. He says his job keeps him away a lot. He works for an oil company."

"And you don't call him during those spells?"

"I can't, because his phone is company-issued and he ..."

"Sinsi, Sinsi."

"What?"

"He disappears for a few days, and you can't call him. You know what that sounds like ..."

"Don't say it! Don't say it! I know, it sounds like he's ..."

"Married."

"I told you not to say it."

"So you've thought about it too."

"I've thought about it, but ..."

"You haven't asked him?"

"Nooooooooooo ..." Sinsi sounds like a little girl admitting she didn't wash her hands before supper.

"Sinsi, you have to know this."

"I know you're right. I'm just so afraid that he will say 'yes.' Or worse yet, that he will say 'no,' and it will be a lie. I should be ashamed of myself, shouldn't I? The only reason I've been able to live with this suspicion is that we haven't slept together yet. So I don't feel guilty being an adulterer or anything like that."

"But, if you keep it up, you know it's going there."

"You're right."

"And even if it doesn't go there, your heart is getting worked over."

"You're right, you're right. I guess it just felt so right—the boys like him so much. I guess I didn't want to burst the bubble."

"I understand that. But, remember what you said the guy has to be right for you, and not just your sons."

"Yeah."

"If he is legally bound to someone else, that's not right for you. Not in the long run, at least."

"Like I said, you're right," she says. Then the floodgates opened.

"Damn!" Sinsi shouts. "I'm tired of this. It's always something, you know? They've got some hang-up, or they live in another state, or they want to be a player, or they think they own you, or they're too broke to take you to the movies, or they've got a drinking problem, or they can't get away from their mama."

"I know."

"Or they can't get it up, or they can't stop getting it up." Sinsi laughs hysterically. "Girl, you know, this is a rough time to be a single black woman! My mother is always telling me, 'You need to get out more and meet some nice men.' I don't have the heart to tell her, 'Mother, I'm trying, but where are they?'"

Thank God Sinsi is a sensible woman, because she will make it her business to get to the bottom of her new boyfriend's unexplained absences and inaccessibility. It could be his job, but Sinsi has to make sure it's not something else keeping them apart. Her sons don't need another scoundrel in their lives, and neither does she.

. . .

Portia, Portia, Portia. That woman is a trip, a Ticker in a class all by herself. Portia looks like the type of woman that would hum in the kitchen while she's baking cakes from scratch. You can just see her tickling her grandbabies and setting her hair in rollers at night, and you imagine fresh white linens on her table and flowers all over her house. She looks homey.

But Portia is no Betty Crocker. She is a straight-talking, no-holds-barred businesswoman, a dentist who runs a popular clinic near Austin, Texas, and a woman who is on the make. She wants a man, and not to hold her hand or keep her company. Portia's motives are purely, unabashedly and unapologetically sexual.

"I need a man for health reasons," she says. "Mental health and physical health. I'm not getting any younger, and if I am going to have anything like a good sex life again, it needs to happen now."

When she turned, 50, Portia thought she had a good 10 years before she had to worry about her sex life. "But in the last five years, things started changing so fast. I'm drooping here, and fattening up there. You wouldn't know it now, but I used to be 'all that.' Now, my sister says, 'You used to be all that; now you're all that and super-sized.'"

She giggles lightly, and then suddenly lowers her voice. "That's not funny, bitch."

Portia is a character, for sure. But she has touched on a fear that many women share—the fear of what aging and maturity will do to a woman in a society that is so hung up on appearances.

"I don't even bother with the young boys, because there's no way they're going to be interested in me," Portia says. "If they are, I know something's wrong. They've got a mommy complex or something. But that's all right. I can handle that. What makes me sick are these guys my age—and even older—who act like they've still got it going on. They want the young girls, too, you know. It's ridiculous, isn't it? You know what I'm talking about."

"Oh, yes. I know what you're talking about."

"Well, what are we going to do about it, Deb? I've got all this experience and all the time in the world now that my kids are finally out of the house. But, you know what gets me? Now that I have all this so-called freedom, I don't have anybody to enjoy it with."

"You still look really good, Portia." She does. Portia has exaggerated her "drooping." She still has quite a figure and a gorgeous pair of legs.

"But I look kind of like a church lady, don't I?"

We scream with laughter.

"You have a very gentle, kind face. And you dress very conservatively. But, no, you don't look matronly, not by any means."

"Maybe I need to get out of these suits. Maybe I need to get some of those low, tight blue jeans, and pierce my navel."

"Please."

"Or let my bra show, and get an ankle bracelet."

"Like my friend Michelle says, those days are over," I say.

"I know it. I'm just teasing. You know if I went out of the house like that I'd get arrested."

"But I know what you're saying about men and looks."

"This new sexual liberation is all well and good, but I sure wish it had come along when I was in my prime. My prime, honey, my prime."

"Supposedly, you're in your prime now."

"Sheeeeeee-it. Tell that to those young honeys who have the men all wrapped up."

"But you shouldn't have a problem finding a man to have sex with, if that's all you want. Women can still get laid."

"You know that's not all I want. It's one of the main things I want, but it's not all I want."

"You're looking for someone to be intimate with in every way, right?"

"Right. That's what I'm trying to say. I want intimacy. That's sex, but not just sex. That's being able to share your heart and soul with a man. That's being able to be yourself with a man."

"When's the last time you had that?"

"Like never."

"Aw, come on. You told me you had a great relationship with Ronnie."

"Yeah, Ronnie was great. But where is he now? Out with wife number three or four, that's where. And how old is she? Twenty-seven."

"I bet you there are times that he wishes he still had you to talk to."

"I don't want to talk! I told you what I want to do."

"Portia ..."

"I'm serious. I went through the period of my life where I wanted to be appreciated for my mind. I proved how successful I was, opened my own practice, got all the degrees, sat on all those boards, and got appointed to governor's task forces. That was fine then. Now I want to be appreciated for the sexpot that I am."

When we finally stop roaring, Portia turns serious for a moment.

"No joke," she says. "I'm really starting to think that if it doesn't happen soon, it may not ever happen again. And yes, I know about all those stories about men and women in the nursing home getting it on, but I want to enjoy sex while I can still shake my own ass a little, rather than it shaking all by itself, you know?

"I'm not joking. It sounds like I am, I know. But in a few years, I won't be laughing."

· 5 ·

Freestylers

W E ALL KNOW WHAT SUPERMAN LOOKS LIKE: He is tall, sturdy, and strong; good looking; our same age, or a couple of years older; earns more money than we do; and wears his blackness with dignity. Everyone knows his character: He is loyal, patient, honest, brave, faithful, and hard-working, and he cares deeply about his loved ones. Everyone knows his personality: Witty, smart, and courteous, with a touch of adventure and mischief. If he comes without a lot of baggage—either no exes, or at least none with drama; no children, or at least no custody messes; no financial binds; and no trouble with the law—well, it doesn't get any better than that.

Let's get real. Superman is as rare as kryptonite. We might keep an eye out for him, but sooner or later, most of us come to grips with the fact that if we really want a relationship, we'll have to whittle down the dream package. Compromise is the name of the game.

There's a lot of debate about how much whittling a self-respecting woman should do. In *Loving Me*, Claudette Sims wrote, "Many sisters feel they have no choice, so even though they're smart, attractive, and successful, they are settling for no-win situations with men who are available, but not necessarily compatible intellectually and socially."

However, psychologist Dr. Julia Hare once issued this caution in an *Ebony* article: "If the black man doesn't have the job, the financial security, and the nice home, then we assume he is not a 'good' black man. But that is not fair. We have forgotten about the spiritual qualities that the UPS driver and other blue-collar men bring to the relationship."

According to some experts, it's not just men on lower rungs of the economic ladder that we tend to overlook, but also men of other race and age groups. The Freestylers already understand this. When the well runs dry, they don't go thirsty. They find another source of water. They have pitched the old rules of engagement—same race, same age, same socio-economic class, same religion, and same country—and widened their options. Not everybody has the stomach for such compromise. But as Billie Holliday sang, "Them that's got, shall get."

. . .

The very idea of hooking up with a white, Latin, or Asian man used to repulse Diane—especially the white men. To her, there was so much heavy historical language ... the whole Sally Hemings thing, and all that business about black women as sexual objects. As psychologists Stephanie Brown and Lily McNair put it, "The image of the lusty, insatiable black woman was a fantasy constructed in the minds of white men."

But on her 30th birthday, Diane accepted a white male coworker's invitation for a celebratory lunch, and was surprised to find herself intrigued. She had already decided that Brian was good looking "in a George Clooney kind of way" and considered him smart, nice, and friendly. But Diane was nervous when she looked Brian in the eye a few hours later in the office.

"I was afraid he could see what I was thinking," Diane says. "What I was thinking was that I would like to be with this guy some more ... kind of like a test drive."

"Why didn't you want him to know?" I ask. "Was it because you worked together, or because he was white?"

"A little of both, I think," Diane says. "I was really uncomfortable. Usually I'm really in control, so I didn't know what to do with what I was feeling."

"Which was animal attraction."

"Oh, yeah, big time."

"How long did you avoid making eye contact?"

"Well, here's the thing. I tried to avoid him for a couple of days, and then on about the third day after my birthday, he jumped on an elevator with me and said, 'We need to talk.' I knew right away what it was about."

"And that was?"

"He wanted to know if I was avoiding him, which I denied, naturally. I gave him some bullshit excuse like, 'I don't want people to start talking because we went to lunch together.' And he said, 'I don't care if they do.'"

"Whoa."

"Whoa is right. I could tell he was going somewhere with this, and that really made me nervous. But I pulled it together—you know I wasn't going to let this white boy shake me—so I looked him dead in his eyes and said, 'Oh, and why don't you care, Brian?' And he got real sexy-sounding, bit his lip, and said, 'These people can't tell me who I want to be with.'"

"Hmm."

"So I said, 'And you want to be with me?' And he said, 'I think so.' That kind of threw me off my game, so I tried to get the upper hand again and put him on the defensive. 'You *think* so? Why don't you *know* so?' He said, 'Because I don't know if you want to be with me.' Girl, you should have seen him. He was smoldering."

Within an hour of that encounter, Diane and Brian set a date for dinner the next evening. Diane says they were "exploring." Apparently, they found something, because that was in 2001, and they've been a couple ever since.

"If you would have told me I would have a white boyfriend for even a minute, let alone for years, I would have thought you were crazy," Diane says. "I didn't have anything against white men ... it's just that they never crossed my mind as potential partners. Even Brian. I was really attracted to him and we had so much in common—around the same age, in the same business, both real serious types—but I didn't think of him in that way until after we came back from lunch that day, and frankly, I had no idea he was thinking of me in that way."

Diane grew up in Illinois and migrated to Washington, D.C., to work on Capitol Hill after college. Over the years, she's had boyfriends off and on—about eight relationships and "semi-relationships," she says—and all of them were with black men.

"I'm generally attracted to tall, strong, serious brothers," Diane says. "And I like them really black, coal black. So, you can see why it blew my mind to be attracted to a guy who is white, although Brian is on the darker side of white."

A couple of times, Diane thought her relationships with black men were on the brink of marriage. One of the men turned out to be a chronic philanderer. "He could not stay faithful, no matter what," Diane recalls. "Sometimes I pretended not to notice; denial, you know. And sometimes I confronted him. We would have these knockdown fights. Mainly I was fighting; he was just kind of sulking in the corner, saying, 'I'm sorry, baby, I'm sorry.' Whenever I would confront him, he wouldn't lie about it, I can give him that much credit. I think that's why I kept holding on—because I believed he had a good heart, just a weak you-know-what."

"How long did this go on?" I ask.

"Two years," says Diane. "Two tough years. Don't ask me why, but I loved the guy. I mean, except for the running around, he was really great. Fine. Very intelligent. Dressed like *GQ*. Treated me like a queen when he wasn't treating me like shit behind my back."

"What brought it to an end?"

"What brought it to an end was when he hit on my cousin at a family reunion. I had taken him to meet the folks, you know. It was that serious. Then the cousin, who is a couple years younger than me—and married, though she came without her husband because he's an asshole—pulls me over that night at dinner and says my boyfriend—almost my fiancé at the time—asked if they could picnic. Can you believe that? That was it."

"So you broke up with him then."

"I broke up with him after we got back to D.C. I was real cool because I didn't want to upset my mother and the rest of the family and ruin the family reunion. But, when we got back, I told him I knew what had happened and, you know what? He didn't even deny it. But that little routine didn't work this time. I told him I was out."

Diane's second brush with commitment came three years later. She met Sean at a popular watering spot in northern Virginia. Diane is convinced that Sean was faithful. In fact, she says, he was so conspicuously crazy about her that she thinks it's possible that he never even looked at other women during their nine months together.

"Sean's problem was self-esteem, I think," says Diane. "He was so insecure that anytime I asked him where he was going or when he would be back, he would get defensive and say I was trying to control him."

"Oh, the control thing," I nod.

"Oh yeah. The control thing. 'I'm a grown man. I don't have to answer to my mama. I sure don't have to answer to you.' That kind of crap. I would ask him, 'Why are you trippin'? All I want to know is when you're coming back.' And he would just go off."

"Did those two bad experiences sour you on black men?" I ask.

"Oh, no, no way," Diane says. "I know there are some good brothers out there. I have three brothers, and they are all great men. My father wasn't much to speak of, but I have an uncle that I think the world of, and my grandfather is like a great king. I've worked with some really good black men. So, no, if anything, I blame myself for making bad choices. I wouldn't paint all black men with one brush."

Diane narrows her eyes. "You're wondering if this is why I'm with a white man?" she asks.

I answer with a shrug.

"Naw, naw. Like I said, I was totally into black men—black, black men. But I like being in a relationship. I like having a man in my life. I wasn't having any real luck, but I wasn't ready to give up yet. It just so happened that this really great guy came along, and he was white. Am I supposed to pass up a chance to be happy because his skin color is different? I don't think so."

"How happy are you?"

"Very happy. Very at peace."

"Where do you think you and Brian are headed?"

"We're probably going to get married in a year."

"Probably?"

"Yeah, we've talked about it. A lot. It's definitely headed that way."

"Why a year? For planning time?"

"Yeah, planning time and just to make sure, you know."

"So you're not quite sure?"

"I'm sure I love Brian, and I'm sure he loves me. It's just that there's more to think about in an interracial relationship. Children, you know. We have to really be sure about this because we really want children, and mixed children have some issues to face. They don't need their parents to be messed up."

One thing Diane is not worried about, she insists, is what other people think about her interracial affair. Not generally. Every now and then, when she's out with Brian, she catches someone staring, and she usually responds by staring back. But it's the looks she sometimes gets from black men that bother her most. "They might look mad, or they might look hurt," Diane says. "And it hurts me to think that they believe I'm rejecting them and choosing a white man over them. That's not it at all. But what can I do, stop and sit them down and explain my relationship? Pass out little cards explaining why Diane is with a white man? You see what I'm saying? You can't live that way. And the bottom line is, it's not their business who I'm with."

"Remember what Brian said? 'I don't care what they think.'"

"Brian was ahead of his time," Diane says, lifting her wine glass. "Here's to Brian."

· · ·

There's no such luck for Carolyn, a 51-year-old registered nurse from Richardson, Texas. Dating white men is just too much work, she says. One man in particular just didn't get it.

"I had to explain so many things that it was like someone was trying to get me to see that we didn't belong together. He didn't know anything about black culture. He didn't know the music, the food, the comedy, the slang … nothing. He had no soul whatsoever. He was nice, but no soul."

Carolyn says the other fellow had a cursory acquaintance with black culture—"the stuff you pick up just by watching TV," she says. But when she was with him, the scornful looks she got from black men were just too much to bear. "You could tell they didn't like it one bit that I was with a white man. Sometimes I could ignore it, and sometimes I couldn't. I finally just stopped seeing him because I didn't want to feel guilty anymore. I was feeling guilty, like I had betrayed black men."

Carolyn is still a Freestyler, but a wary one, at least where race is concerned. After two bad experiences, she decided that she and white men are not compatible, and she's crossed them off her list. Asian men are out, too, "because they're basically white men from another part of the world." She might consider a Latino man, "if he's brown enough," but what she really wants is a black partner. And there's the problem: there don't seem to be many around—not in her age range, at least, and she won't compromise on the age issue. "They've got to be from my generation," she says.

Disillusioned, Carolyn is gradually becoming a Shrinker. She has cut back on social outings and is turning into a homebody. If she meets the right man, it will have to be an act of chance or by a bolt of fate. "I don't have the time or the energy to go on a big manhunt," she says.

She'd better hope her cable goes out.

. . .

Then there's Sabrina, a 31-year-old New Yorker who works in the financial services industry. She's never married, and she's never been close, she says. Sabrina finds the shortage of black men lamentable, but she's not really fazed by it because she's come to the conclusion that she's more comfortable with white men.

That may be because she grew up in Palo Alto, California, a predominantly white, middle-class college town. It's not just any college town, either: it's Stanford's town. Sabrina's parents were part of Palo Alto's "in crowd;" they sent their daughter to great schools and kept her comfortable in a pleasant, middle-class neighborhood. Her exposure to the black community was limited, to put it mildly.

"I remember my first crush," she says. "I was in the second grade, and this boy had sandy brownish blond hair and fierce blue eyes. I thought he was so cute." That was the beginning. Looking back, Sabrina realizes that most of the men she's ever been attracted to and related to were white.

"For the most part, I've dated white men, with just a sprinkling of black men," Sabrina says. She thinks she disappointed her black dates because she wasn't "down" enough for them. None of them clicked.

Sabrina is now involved with a man she has known since her childhood. When he moved to New York, they reconnected and a romance blossomed. She thinks they might get married eventually … at least, she wouldn't be surprised if they did. His race—his whiteness—isn't an issue at all. "Respect, consideration, open-mindedness, a willingness to listen—these are what really matter to me most," says Sabrina. It helps that her man has a similar education to hers and makes a good living, like she does, because Sabrina has no intention of living beneath her accustomed standards.

Should the relationship fail, Sabrina is not averse to dating a black man, but she is skeptical about the prospects of it working out. Most of the brothers she meets are either from a different world than hers, or they're into white women, which, ironically, bothers Sabrina on general principle.

"Part of me always thinks, 'There are so few of them.' If they were abundant, it might not bother me so much. But when I know there's so few of them … wow—that's tough. It's another slap in the face, telling you that you're not good enough."

Yet Sabrina doesn't see her choice as having the same effect, necessarily. It's more practical and personal than that. "It really shouldn't matter," Sabrina says, speaking of race. "What's the ultimate goal? To be happy, right? Just be happy."

. . .

The stereotype goes something like this: If a man in his 50s or 60s is with a woman in her 20s or 30s, his mind has been blown by the poontang, and he is probably paying for it, literally and liberally. The same prejudice applies to the older woman with a younger man. But as we look at the older man with cynicism and even disgust—"Look at him, old fool, with that young girl"—we tend to look at the older woman with pity. "Bless her heart. She must really be lonely."

A lot of black women are saying "to hell with that" these days. If they meet a man who makes them happy—in whatever way and for whatever reasons—and he happens to be younger, even much younger, why not give it a shot? As L.A. Johnson wrote in a 2005 *Pittsburgh Post-Gazette* article, "In 1997, at least 117,000 of 4.1 million unmarried couples nationwide were women with men at least 10 years younger, and at least 262,000 of the 53 million married couples were women married to men at least 10 years younger, Census figures show. In 2003, at least 421,000 of 4.6 million unmarried couples were women with men at least six years younger, and at least 2.3 million of the 58 million married couples were women married to men at least six years younger."

The old rule may not be broken yet, but it's bending, and the Freestylers are stomping on it in the name of love.

. . .

Anthony must have been something. You can tell by the way Rochelle's 44-year-old face softens and her eyes twinkle when she talks about him. "He was a doll," she purrs. "And he was so much fun." He was also 14 years younger than she was.

They met over a pile of receipts and files and government forms.

Rochelle had decided to have an accounting service prepare her income taxes that year, since she had bought a new house and wanted to make sure her finances were correctly reported. During Rochelle's first visit to the accounting firm, she was helped by an older, humorless woman. When she returned a few days later to retrieve her completed forms, Anthony led her into his cubicle.

"You couldn't help but notice his eyes," she says. "They were so deep-set, and he had the prettiest eyelashes. And nice, white, straight teeth. His smile was beautiful. That's the first thing I noticed."

But there was more. Tight butt. Strong arms. Great cologne. And, most of all, he had a smooth, sexy, cool style—what Rochelle thought Denzel Washington must be like.

"When I think back on it, I realize I was probably flirting with him," says Rochelle. "It took about an hour to go over everything—I wanted a full explanation, you understand—and the whole time, I was crossing and uncrossing my legs, we were laughing, I was touching his arms, and he was touching my arm."

"How old did you think he was?" I ask. "Could you tell?"

"I didn't know exactly how young he was, but I knew that he was a lot younger than I was," Rochelle says. "It ran through my mind a couple of times that I ought to be ashamed of myself, but not for long. No, ma'am. He erased that thought right out of my head, especially when he moved in for the kill."

"And how did he do that?"

"Well," she says, sinking back into her chair and softening her face. "When I got ready to pay the fee, he gave me the total and told me how pleased he was that it was lower than I expected."

"And?"

"And he said, 'Oh, you've got to have enough left to take me out to dinner.'"

"Uh-huh."

"So," says Rochelle, licking her lips. "I said, 'I would love to take you out to dinner. Why don't you call me some time? You have my number in your files.' He said he would."

"And he did, right?"

"To tell you the truth, I didn't really expect him to. I thought he was just giving me that line, you know. But the next day, when I got home from work, there was a call from him on my voicemail."

"How soon did you call him back?"

"Not right away. I had to stop screaming first. And I had to call my girlfriends and tell them, 'Girl, this sweet young thing from the accounting firm is hitting on me.' I told them all about the going-out-to-dinner conversation."

"What did your girlfriends say?"

"Well, one of them was more excited than I was. She said, 'Go for it.' The other one said she would support whatever I decided and that she guessed it couldn't hurt anything, but she also warned me to be careful, because young guys can be slick. They have screwed-up ideas about older women. For sure, I didn't want to play mommy to any grown man."

Rochelle and Anthony had dinner one night about a week later. He paid. Afterward, he and Rochelle talked for hours at her house. They kissed. Rochelle melted. So did her reservations. They had two other dates in the next week—both at Rochelle's house. On their fourth date, Rochelle and Anthony went to bed together. That did it.

"I would say we had two or three months of this intense, fun, exciting May-December romance before he pretty much moved into my house," Rochelle says. "I was on cloud nine. Everybody asked me, 'What's going on?' They kept telling me that my complexion looked good, my body looked good, and my hair looked good. I guess it was the glow. I know I felt like I was glowing."

But at about the six-month mark, when some of the initial novelty and passion had begun to fade, the age difference raised its worrisome head. It showed in major ways, and in little ones.

Rochelle is divorced, a respected educator with a retirement plan ripening in the wings and twin 26-year-old daughters. Anthony was an accountant who dreamed of being a music producer. He liked to tinker with mixing boards in makeshift studios in his spare time. Rochelle's idea of a good time was to get home in time for *Jeopardy*, have a light dinner and a shower, and get to bed by 10; Anthony was a night owl who liked to go out almost every night and thought 2 a.m. was an appropriate bedtime. Rochelle liked Angela Winbush and Chaka Khan on her stereo; Anthony listened to Nas, Nelly, and 50 Cent at full blast. Rochelle wanted to vacation in Tuscany; Anthony had his eye on South Beach.

"You could just feel the generation gap," Rochelle says. "I was nearly twice his age. My girlfriend—the one who held back when I first told her about Anthony—now thinks that Anthony has been really good for me. When I tell her about some of the problems, she tells me it wouldn't hurt for me to loosen up some. She's probably right, but I can't turn back the hands of time. I'm not interested in reinventing myself. Anthony was 30, but I wasn't."

Eventually, Rochelle's young accountant peeled off. He moved out, saying that he didn't want to look like a gigolo who was "kept" by a woman. Gradually, his visits and calls to Rochelle's house decreased. Finally, after a two-week-long disappearing act, Anthony announced that the woman he had broken up with shortly before meeting Rochelle—a woman in her mid-20s, around the age of Rochelle's daughters—had moved back to town, and he was seeing her again.

"Well, I wasn't about to share him," says Rochelle as she leans forward, her eyebrows arching. "I told Anthony that I was disappointed in him, that I didn't think it was too demanding of me to expect honesty and faithfulness, that I had always been that way with him, and that I expected him to be straight with me, to be a man. He said, 'I'm not trying to settle down. You knew I was a young man when you met me.' Are you believing this?"

Rochelle is now dating a man who is her age. He's dependable. He's classy. He shares many of Rochelle's interests. "And he bores me to tears," she says. "Isn't that a terrible thing to say? See, that's the real downside of dating a man a lot younger than you: They're exciting. It's hard to go back to the old settled-down guys who have to take glucosamine everyday. Or Viagra! William's not like that, really … that's not fair. But, child, he ain't Anthony!"

Rochelle believes she will eventually find a man who fits her. Despite her unhappy ending with Anthony, she believes that Mr. Right could be a much younger man. "If you're a black woman, and you're serious about finding a soul mate, you have to make some compromises these days," she says. "You used the word 'settling' before. I don't think of it as settling. I think of it as being flexible. If you don't consider younger men, you're leaving out a huge segment of the male population. That's only cheating yourself."

"Sounds like you're making the case for older women and younger men," I respond.

"Not necessarily. I can't tell you that I'm going to find another young man, because I'm not out and about where they usually are. But if another guy comes along who rings my bell, I'm not going to ignore him just because he's younger than me."

But from now on, says Rochelle, she is doing her own taxes.

. . .

Jackie, 36, works in the public-relations department of a major Atlanta-based corporation. She's been doing a serious nutrition and exercise program for the past few years and has developed a decent golf game. Between her leisure activities and her job, she is often found on the social scene with an array of interesting, accomplished men. Getting "booked"—getting dates—has never been a problem for Jackie. But finding "the one" has been a royal pain.

"I talked myself out of certain things, like 'He must have a graduate degree, like me,' 'He must own his own home,' or, 'He must work out.' I convinced myself that all that stuff was superficial and really didn't matter, but I was still having a hard time finding someone who was a good fit for me, " Jackie says.

One night, Jackie visited a friend's art studio for a showing and reception. Afterward, she was drawn into a debate about "what is black art" with a group of people who'd stuck around after the reception. Some of the talk was bunk and bull, "people just trying to sound deep," Jackie says. But a handsome, well-dressed young man on a nearby settee impressed her. Jackie found herself agreeing with most of what he said and falling for his cool, intelligent reasoning. He had a sense of humor and a killer smile.

"I could not *believe* how interested I was in this man, you know? I could tell he was younger, but I could just feel myself kind of melting anyway. Eventually, he saw it too, because we kept doing that eye dance—you know what I'm talking about—and he really started flirting with me, and damned if I didn't flirt back."

Nearly a year after their meeting, Jackie is still sounding surprised by her reaction to Chris, a 26-year-old event planner and promoter.

By the end of the first night at the art studio, Jackie and Chris exchanged phone numbers and e-mail addresses. They've been a couple ever since, and Jackie thinks marriage might be in the picture.

"I still have to get my mind around being nine years older than him until death do we part," Jackie says. "But he makes me laugh, and he makes me think, and he makes me feel good all the time."

Jackie realizes that age difference can be a problem for some women, but she cautions her fellow Sole Sisters against setting a hard-and-fast rule against dating younger men.

"You don't know what you may be missing," she says. "There's a possibility that they're too immature or too insecure or not ready for you. But, there's also a possibility that your mind is not as old as your body, and that he is older than his years. Either way, it's all about how the two of you get along. If it's right, age shouldn't get in the way at all."

. . .

You may remember that old Moms Mabley line: "Ain't nothing an old man can do for me but bring me a message from a young man." For Yvonne, 30, that wasn't just a joke; it was a credo. Like a lot of women, she'd never been interested in considerably older men—the "Old Spice-and-Desenex" crowd, as Yvonne calls them.

"Four years older. That was my limit," she says. "Not five years, four years. That kept us in the same general range, but gave him a little bit of an edge on me. I liked that. But, girl, it's drying up out there. The young men are too busy chasing ass and trying to get into the NBA. The middle-aged men are married or maybe divorced because they were so full of shit. There are some good young ones and some good middle-aged ones too. And there are some old dogs. But if you're trying to meet someone, I realize now that you can't count out the Old Spice-and-Desenex crowd."

She agreed to go out with Travis because he was so polite and liked to do things first-class. There were other reasons, too: because he attends church—he's a deacon—and because he smells like soap.

"I take it he's single?" I ask.

"Oh, yeah. Divorced. Long time, something like 20 years."

"And he never remarried?"

"He said he thought about it once, but the woman was kind of schizoid. You know, kind of loopy, lots of drama. So they broke up."

"What does he do? Does he still work?"

"Works for the state."

"And how did the two of you meet?"

"He was a customer. I helped him pick out a tennis bracelet for his daughter's graduation—she was getting her master's degree—and I could tell he was kind of interested in me, but I wasn't interested in him, so I just played it off."

"So how did the two of you connect?"

"He came back a couple of days later and said that he was worried that his daughter already had a tennis bracelet. I thought he was probably lying, just looking for an excuse to come back, but I waited on him for over an hour and helped him find the right thing for his daughter. He got her a really nice pair of diamond earrings."

"Ooh, generous."

"I know. That's what I thought too. Well, anyway, by the time he left it was like we were old friends. He said he wanted to take me out to dinner because he appreciated how patient I had been with him. Then he gave me this little wink, and I knew."

"Apparently you were interested enough to give him your number."

"Not really. I mean, I thought he was really nice looking, but like I said, I wasn't into older men. But he was nice, and polite, and we had gotten along so well, I figured it couldn't hurt for me to give him my number. I wasn't worried about him harassing me or anything."

"When did he call?"

"The same night! You hear me? That same night. Brother Man wasted no time."

"And he asked you out then?"

"After about an hour on the phone, yeah. I figured, why not?"

Travis chose one of the city's nicest restaurants for his first date with Yvonne—the kind of place that requires men to wear jackets, and the waiters brush away the crumbs as soon as they fall. The kind of place that doesn't list prices on the menu.

"The conversation was great, and he was such a gentleman," Yvonne says. "I found out all about his first marriage, how his wife had drinking and gambling problems. They had two kids, who are grown now, of course: a son and a daughter. She's the one he bought the earrings for. He also has a young grandson. All of them live here, in Detroit."

When they'd finished eating and talking, Yvonne and Travis moved on to a popular bar down the street from the restaurant. At the bar, there was live music and a jumping crowd on the dance floor.

"I didn't think he would be the dancing type, but he asked me almost as soon as we walked in the door," Yvonne remembers. "Lord, what did I do that for?"

"What do you mean?" I ask.

"It was kind of embarrassing," Yvonne says. "Travis dances old-school. I'm talking 'bout *real* old-school. He had a jitterbug thing going on." Yvonne laughs until she chokes.

"People were looking at us, like, what is this? Lawrence Welk or some shit? But I don't think he noticed. He was too busy cutting up. I have to admit I felt uncomfortable because we just stood out so much."

"Because of the dancing, and not the age difference?"

"Exactly. Travis is old enough to be my dad—he's 26 years older than me. But he could pass for younger. And I don't dress like most 30-year-olds and I sure don't act like most 30-year-olds, so I think I probably blend in with him better than you might think. Don't get me wrong: you can tell he's older than me, but he's tall, strong, handsome, and kind of suave, you know, so he doesn't look like a pathetic old man trying to act like he's 30, with a young thang on his arm. To answer your question, no, I don't think it was shocking for people to see us together."

"So, it was just the dancing that drew attention to you?"

"Yeah, the daaaaaaaancing."

"You sounded kind of mushy when you were describing Travis."

"I did? Well, I'm not mushy about him, but I might be getting that way."

"Oh, really?"

"He's great to me. I mean, really great. But …"

"But what?"

"It's just that I want to get married and have kids one day. I mean, we are really good together, and Travis is in really good shape. But, he is in his late 50s, and I'm just getting to my 30s. By the time I'm his age, I could be a widow. I don't mean to sound cold about it, but that's the truth. If we have kids, I'd have them all by myself. I'm just saying that that's something I have to think about."

Yvonne is not dating anyone other than Travis. That has given the relationship a serious feel, and Yvonne's friends and family have picked up on it. Her mother is nervous, her brothers and sisters are opposed to the romance, and Yvonne's best friend, Malesha, thinks she's missing opportunities to meet men her own age.

"They all get on my nerves," says Yvonne. "There's no way they can understand what's going on in my relationship, and it's none of their business anyway. Except my mom—I do feel bad about that. I keep trying to tell her that I'm all right, and that I know what I'm doing. But you know how mothers can be. She wants to make sure I'm happy. I just wish she would trust that I know what I'm doing."

"Do you?"

"Do I know how this is going to end up? No. But, for right now,

I'm satisfied. And if it goes further than that, then so be it. I can say this much: I'm not apologizing because Travis is older than me. You take love where you can get it. I didn't plan to be with someone almost twice my age, but that's how it is."

. . .

To hear some brothers tell it, black women are all about money: the bling-bling and getting paid. I wish I had a dollar for every time I've heard that one. Maybe this is why the black marriage rate is down. Black women are outgunning black men in jobs and in income. Single black women are finishing college, going to graduate school, moving into management positions, and buying their own homes—and leaving single black men in the dust.

Maybe that's why some men think money and material goods are what matters most to black women. They're misconstruing the fact that single black women are moving on with their lives and acquiring what used to be common only among the married to be a statement of values and, in some cases, a declaration of disinterest in men who can't match their achievements.

"Men accuse them of being materialistic because they're high-fashion women who live in nice surroundings," explained Dr. Gwendolyn Goldsby Grant, a psychologist and sex counselor, in a July 2002 interview with the Morris News Service. "Men measure their manhood by their paycheck."

There are certainly sisters who will not consider a relationship with men below their socioeconomic station. Some are adamant about it. And it's not unconscionable for an accomplished woman to prefer an accomplished man, and vice versa. At the same time, the widening disparities in education, employment, and income between black women and black men mean that black women who stick to that standard are going to find slim pickings. Historically, black women have not let the education gap stand in the way of a good relationship. Research has shown that among married black couples, wives are more likely than not to have more education than their husbands.

As the shortage of available men grows, more and more women are Freestyling these days and ignoring the idea that a man must be at least their social, educational, and economic equal.

"I don't believe that a woman who earns more than her mate is entering into a recipe for failure," remarked hip-hop writer and author Bakari Kitwana in an interview on the Urban Think Tank's website. "I think it's up to the individuals to wade through the complexities and not stoop to society's often low expectations of black men and women."

. . .

Gail prefers men with impressive careers, considerable education, and handsome incomes. Of course she does. As a well-respected lawyer in Milwaukee, she commands a six-figure income, works in a private office with a view, drives a Lexus, and wears St. John suits. For the past 10 years, Gail has spent her vacation time at exclusive spas and has traveled internationally, unwinding in such lush locales as Tuscany, Monte Carlo, and Barcelona. A live-in housekeeper and nanny allows Gail, 43 and divorced, to focus on her job while juggling two young children, a love of tennis, an occasional stint in community theater, and advocacy work as a board member of a nonprofit literacy organization.

She had hoped for a male version of herself, but found them to be scarce as hen's teeth. "I kept looking in one direction for the magic, but I wasn't having any luck," Gail says.

Along came Reggie. At 42, he's a year younger than Gail. He's not what Gail had in mind: a lawyer, a doctor, or maybe a professor. Reggie works as a security guard at the airport.

"It bothered me a lot at first," says Gail. "Then it started bothering me that it bothered me. It was so 'bourgie' of me. I believe that you have to have your standards, but that one was stuck-up, and I knew it. I like to say that Reggie charmed me right out of my stupidity. The old me wouldn't have given him the time of day."

"What happened to the old Gail?" I ask.

"I got tired of not having anyone in my life," she says. "The kind of man I thought I wanted didn't seem to exist. A lot of guys who seemed good turned out to be dogs, or they were threatened by me. Or they didn't read or follow politics. Or they didn't want to go anywhere. It was always something."

She's white-collar and he's blue-collar, but Gail says it's a shallow distinction. "I met this man who didn't seem to be right, and for some reason, something told me to pay attention to him. Sure enough, he turned out to be what I was looking for. I'd just been looking for love in all the wrong places. Isn't that how the song goes?"

"What if he had been younger?" I ask.

"I might have paid attention—as long as he wasn't too much younger," Gail replies.

"What if he had been older?"

"No problem, but not too old."

"And how old is too old?"

"Fifty. No, 55. No, 50."

"Fifty is only seven years older than you."

"I know. But you know men age differently. I don't want to have to deal with all that midlife stuff until I get there with him."

"What if Reggie had been white, Latin, or Asian?"

"Nope. Not going there."

"Why not?"

"I want somebody who understands that part of my existence. I don't want to have to bring them up to speed or teach them about certain things. He's got to be a brother. I know he gets it."

"I'm assuming you make more money than Reggie, since you're a lawyer."

"Oh, God, yes."

"Not a problem?"

Gail smiles knowingly. She gets that kind of question all the time. "You know, I thought it would be, but it's not," she says. "He makes a pretty decent living, so he can cover all of his expenses and still dress nice, pay for dinner, and take me on vacation. In fact, anytime I try to pay the tab he puts up a fight."

"Is that an ego thing with him?"

"No, I don't get that feeling. He relents every now and then when I pull out my credit card. He doesn't seem offended or embarrassed. Not at all. I just think he wants me to know that he can take care of business too."

"Sounds like a winner," I say.

"So far," she says. "Yep."

Damn, she looks happy.

. . .

Despite some women's successful trips off the beaten path of relationships, it is not for naught that the rules exist. Even if they are hidebound, the idea is to enhance the prospects for compatibility. Supposedly, the closer a man and woman are in age, experience, habits, and lifestyle, the better the chances are that they'll make a good match.

You can manipulate the rules, but you can't throw them all out the window. At least I couldn't. But once upon a time, I tried.

The guy was different from me across the board. A different age (much younger), a different race (Arab), a different nationality (Turkish), a different education level (the equivalent of tenth grade), and a different income (broke). But he was the finest thing I had ever seen in my life, and that includes all the men in the movies. He was charming, too.

What won me over, though, was his heart. He was pure and sweet. Once, when he was considering moving to America to be with me, he asked, "What kind of work could I do?" Moments later, a team of sanitation workers appeared on the television screen, and he said, "I could do that." I studied him a moment to see if he was kidding, and when I determined that he wasn't, I said, "Those are garbage collectors. You don't want to do that." He said, "Why not? Work is work." He may as well have been Aristotle. I liked the absence of false pride and the willingness to get his hands dirty if that's what it took to pull his weight.

There were other goodies. He told me that if I lived with him in his hometown in southern Turkey, he couldn't promise me a fancy house, but he would see to it that I was well cared for. "One happy room," he said. "That's all we need."

In this country, the dollar is almighty. Men are often measured—and measure themselves—by how many dollars they have. They often break the bank and their backs to show off their buying power for big houses, fancy cars, and tailored clothes. You have to worry about stepping on their egos, which are really delicate as eggshells despite all their bluster. After all that, a man who says, "work is work" and "one happy room" can sound refreshingly, wonderfully, and bewitchingly sober. He called me "aşkim," or "my love."

For a time, I was not only about to kiss off the rules but my entire life history. I seriously considered becoming the crazy American by the sea, strange but happy with her dashing, young, penniless, and oh-so-earnest man. Why not? After all, I had raised my children and paid my dues. Now it was my time.

For several months, Uğur and I carried on a hot transcontinental love affair. If I had any reservations, it was not about income or culture or education or national differences; instead, it was about the age gap. In my opinion, a man who has survived life in the Third World is, in effect, older than a man of the same age who grew up in privileged America, but I didn't like being closer to his parents' age than to his. It took a visit to his hometown to make that concern vanish.

There, in that beautiful seaside village, his whole family—his mother, father, older sister, sickly older brother and two nieces—received me warmly and treated me like long-lost kin. For three days, we hurdled the language barrier and kept constant company, laughing, shopping, eating, and hugging. Lots of hugging.

Uğur's mother insisted that I call her "anne," the Turkish word for "mama," and when we left on the third day, she cried like a baby, saying, "Don't go, Deborah. Don't go." I felt like I belonged to that family. And I felt like I belonged with Uğur.

Ultimately, it was the culture barrier that did us in. The visit had left his parents longing for their son. They wanted him to leave Istanbul and move back to the small southern village by the sea. Uğur didn't want to go. There were no jobs there. Everyone was poor, and modernity had passed the place by. Many of the prevailing customs—especially where men and women were concerned—were thousands of years old.

"Then, don't go," I counseled.

"You don't understand, aşkim," he said in that sexy accent. "My parents have called me back. This is my culture. I don't have a choice. You can't change culture."

"But you're a grown man. You're entitled to your own life," I declared.

"Aşkim, if I don't go, I will shame my family. All of those people will talk about Sebahat and Yusef's bad son."

"Omigod."

"If you come with me, we will have to be married, but we cannot show affection in front of other people. This is how it is."

"You've got to be kidding me."

"And then they will want babies."

"Who will want babies?"

"My mother and father."

"Uğur, I'm not having any more children. I'm almost 50 years old!"

"If we do not, then everyone will be saying, 'Where are the babies?' If we do not have any children, they will say I have a cursed seed."

For all I knew, this was a crock of bullshit, but Uğur seemed as painfully sincere as ever. Not that it mattered. Love's triumph over age, culture, race, socioeconomic background, and nationality fell flat. I returned to the U.S. heartbroken and shell-shocked but glad that I was old as I was, for once. Had I been younger, I might not have come to my senses. I might be writing this book from some little seaside hut with a passel of babies underfoot, waiting for their street-hustling father to return home with the evening grub and keep his proper distance from me.

Lawd!

I don't regret the experience. It was thrilling for a while. I am sad that it ended because I don't know when, if ever, I will feel those thrills again. I know this: I'm not very good at Freestyling. I think it's best to hang with the Shrinkers, where at least I don't have to put my heart on the line. That's it, you know. Freestylers take chances, Shrinkers like to play it safe, even when that means not playing at all.

· 6 ·

Naw Naws

T HEY TELL ME that there are black women out there who have no interest in men. I'm not talking about either gay women or nuns. These are straight, uncommitted women. Women who are not married, have never been, and don't ever want to be. Women who have no boyfriends, don't date, are content to live alone, are fine with abstinence, and are perfectly comfortable with the prospect of spending the rest of their lives that way.

No one can say how many of these women there are. There could be hundreds, thousands, even millions. But I can say that they are hard to find. Almost every woman I know is at least agreeable to the idea of a mate, even if only an occasional one.

Don't get me wrong. I know plenty of women who would never say that they "need" a man. I'm one of them, in fact. Here's my philosophy: A woman's life is like a cake. With the right ingredients and baked at the right temperature and for the right amount of time, the cake can be delicious on its own. Icing is optional, but it should be sweet and light. Otherwise, why bother? Why not just eat it as it is?

The icing, of course, is the man. Who needs sour, heavy icing?

But not wanting a man, not even considering icing—actually preferring to be manless—that's something else entirely.

· · ·

As a 40th birthday gift to herself, Tamera chose celibacy. She had not exactly been "out there" to begin with, but she'd decided that sex had become more trouble than pleasure, so Tamera shut it down. If she has any doubts about the decision she made six years ago, there's no hint of it in her voice. Her sermon on celibacy is straightforward and eloquent.

"I grew tired of the games and all the work it took, considering it never went anywhere," she says. "I may have felt good during sex, but I hardly ever felt good after sex, because my expectations were not met. I don't mean sexually. I mean emotionally. These men didn't seem capable of making a commitment to be monogamous or, if they could, they would act as if they got forced into it. It didn't seem to matter that I was making the same commitment to them."

The first six months were easy, Tamera says. She came to understand what people meant about how sexual energy might be channeled in directions other than the groin.

"I moved that energy into other things, like poetry. I was always told that I had a poet's soul, but it wasn't until I became celibate that I was able to tap into that creative spirit. I also got healthy. Stopped eating meat. Started drinking only water. I fast for one full day every three months. The new lifestyle cleansed both my body and my mind."

Tamera admits that around the one-year mark, she became "itchy" for sex. "The dreams, oh my goodness, the dreams. Every night I would wake up from another dream of being in bed with a man. I knew it was a sign that some part of me still was longing for that connection. I almost gave into it a couple of times. But before I did, I would think about the day after, and the day after that. I wasn't blaming men. The ones I was attracted to generally had good intentions. But I kept thinking about all those good intentions that went down the drain, and I'm just not up for that anymore."

Tamera plowed into her poetry and work—she's a real estate agent in upstate New York—and dismissed the dreams, which, she says, stopped after about three months.

"I was so proud of myself," she squeals. "What I had really given myself for my 40th birthday was willpower. Celibacy was just a part of that. I was really proud that when it got rough, my willpower held."

Since then, Tamera has reached another conclusion. She can do without sex, and she can do without men altogether. She doesn't despise them—she still values a host of male friends and colleagues—she just doesn't want them too close.

"I'm on a whole different operating level now," she says. "I'm not trying to make a statement as a feminist—I am a feminist, but this is not about advancing any feminist agenda. I'm not saying that this is the right way for anybody other than myself. But I have been so much happier and so much more at peace since I took men out of the equation. My work has improved, and my health has improved. My peace of mind has improved. I'm healthier. I'm productive. I think I'm more fun. I don't want to mess with that."

"Forgive me for playing devil's advocate here," I said. "But what if a truly spectacular man was interested in you?"

"That's already happened. I told you I came close to violating my celibacy a couple times."

"So you just let a good one get away?"

"No, I just sent a good one away. It was my choice, not an accident."

"But let's say he really fit your life. Had all of the right qualifications, he …"

"Nope, nope, nope."

"Let me finish. He had all of the right qualifications, didn't disturb your peace in any way, you were sure you could trust him, and he added something to your life."

"Sorry. It would never get that far."

"So even Mr. Perfect couldn't …"

"There is no Mr. Perfect."

"You know what I mean. As perfect as he could be for you."

"If he's truly perfect for me, he will be content with being my friend."

"And you really mean that."

"I've really meant it for almost seven years now."

What can I say? Everybody ain't able.

. . .

Gwen pulls no punches. "I can't stand men," she says. "They are all dogs. Even the supposed-to-be good ones have some dog in them."

"Good grief," I say. "Sounds like you've been bitten."

"I have been. Two husbands and I don't-know-how-many-boyfriends? Dogs, dogs, dogs, you hear me? Dogs."

"Maybe you've just gotten a bad batch, so to speak."

"Hmph. It's not just me. All of my girlfriends? My sisters? My aunties? Their men are all dogs too."

"Apparently they don't see it that way."

"Oh, yes they do, too. But they don't want to give up their house or have to fight over the kids. My aunties, they're just way too tired and out of it to get back out and start dating again. They're not like that anyway. They would just sit in the house and dry up, crying all day about 'What am I gonna do now?' Uh-uh. Time out for that."

Something must have happened. Gwen must've had a really bad encounter to have drawn such an extreme conclusion and to be so hell-bent against men. I take a stab at it.

"What one thing was the turning point for you?"

"You mean when did I decide that all men are dogs? When I was a little girl."

"No. When did you decide that you hate men and are through with them?"

"About two, three years ago."

"What brought you to that decision?"

"A lot of different things. But if there's only one I had to choose, it would be Ed … Ed-waaaard. He finally made me see that men are shit."

Gwen met Ed on the job at a major overnight delivery company. They were both drivers. According to Gwen, Ed was not the best-looking guy she had ever seen. "He was on the short side, real skinny, and his head looked too big for his body," she says with a scowl. But Ed was polite and charming, and Gwen began seeing him after work.

"My friends would tease me all the time. 'Girl, what are you doing with that little runt? What can he do for you?' That kind of thing. I didn't like it, but I really couldn't argue with them. He *was* a runt. But I still kept going out with him and, like I told them, I appreciated what he was about. All of us had done the fine, six-pack, GQ guys and gotten dogged out big-time by them. Like I told them, Ed was good to me. Real good to me."

Ed became aware of the ribbing Gwen was getting at a friend's party one night. He overheard one of Gwen's friends tell her that she shouldn't have brought Ed along, because her brother had invited a group of friends to the party, and at least one of them wanted to meet Gwen. "She said, 'Why did you bring the runt? I told you I wanted to hook you up with this dude.' We were in the kitchen, but when I stepped out, Ed was standing right there. I could tell by the look on his face that he had heard what she said."

"What did Ed do?"

"Nothing. He just looked real sad the whole night. I kept asking, 'What's wrong?' but he just said, 'I'm all right,' and we just left it at that. But I knew that he had heard her, and he knew that I knew."

"So, no scene? No shouting? No accusations?"

"Nothing. He never said anything about it. I couldn't stand it. I knew he was hurt, so I really turned it on then, girl. I gave him all my attention, all of my time. I told him how handsome he was, and how smart he was. I kept saying how glad I was to have him."

"That must have made him feel better."

"Yeah. Too good, as it turned out."

"What do you mean?"

"Well, I kept doing the 'you're so wonderful' thing. I just kept it going. Built it into my routine, you know what I'm saying? After a while, I noticed that he started to get kind of cocky about it. We'd have a fight, and he would say something like, 'You're lucky to have me,' or, 'A lot of women wish they had a man like me.' And I'm like,

'Oh, no. No, you are not trippin' like that!' Then one time after a fight, he storms out, slams the door, and flies off in his car. I didn't hear from him for two days. I called him on his cell phone and got his voicemail. I went looking for him and couldn't find him."

"What about at work?"

"Oh, we were on different shifts by this time, so I didn't see him at work. I showed up at the start of his shift one day, but I guess he didn't come in, or he sneaked in, because I didn't see him then, either."

"How did it all end up?"

"I found out that he was shacking up with somebody, and get this—it was the sister of the girl who was running him down. My supposed friend! She was hooking them up."

"Good grief."

"Good grief, nothing. Bullshit. Here I am, trying to make this punk feel better about his sorry little ass, and he's out hitting the sister of some skank who's been talking about him like he had a tail. I swear to God, that was *it* for me."

"Well, I can't blame you for that one, my sister," I said.

"I know you can't. Who's going to be fronted off and played like that?"

"But, Gwen. No more men?"

"No more. Not for me. No way. If a piece of nothing like Ed can dog me out, then what are the prime cuts going to do? I'm better off by myself—just me, my little house, my little job, and my rundown car. I don't have to worry about anybody else's laundry, what he eats, if he ate, where he goes, his feelings, his stupid ego, what he wants to do on Saturday night, who's gonna pay for the phone bill … none of that. I know it sounds hard, but I don't want them, period. The rest of y'all can have 'em all, as far as I'm concerned. No more dogs for me unless they're the barking kind."

· 7 ·

Coasters

I DARE SAY that if a single black woman could choose her "type," she would fall in with the Coasters. It's the attitude that sets them apart. Coolness, patience, and perspective are their specialties. They take the shortage of mating prospects in stride. It doesn't bother them anymore than living in the blizzard belt bothers die-hard Minnesotans. It's just a condition, something that is. "No need getting stressed about it," they say. "What will be will be."

This is not to say that they are pleased with the situation, or that they've been spared its sting. There's some heartache, loss, and disappointment in the mix. But these are glass-half-full women; they are optimists. One way or another, things are going to be all right for them. Coasters are also some of the most philosophical single sisters.

. . .

Rosalyn is a successful woman whose life has been full of travel adventures, beautiful homes, and luxe clothes. Despite her career and financial success, she often wishes she had taken a different course. She's fundamentally an old-fashioned girl who wanted a career and more—she also wanted a husband and children. She knows she would have been a terrific mother, and she thinks she would have been a pretty damn good wife, too.

Early on, it looked promising. "I had a four-year relationship with a true renaissance man from Philadelphia," she recalls. "He had done the Holy Cross and Yale thing. He was a scuba diver and a skier. He was well respected by his peers, and a contributor to the community. If there was anybody I ever wanted to be married to, it was him."

But Rosalyn's beloved died young, leaving her despondent and certain she'd never find another like him. She didn't. But she did fall in love again, this time with a man from Atlanta who had a "good background." Just before Rosalyn turned 30, they got engaged.

"I wanted to be a kept woman ... you know: the house in suburbia, the kids. I didn't want to be a career woman. I had one foot in traditionalism and one foot in women's liberation. My father had always treated my mother and me like we were queens. He took care of everything. That's what I wanted, too. It wasn't so much about having the world's greatest love affair. I pretty much followed my mother's philosophy which was, find someone who loves you, and you'll learn to love him."

Unfortunately, Rosalyn's new man turned out to be an under-achiever. "He wasn't very ambitious," Rosalyn says. The relationship ran out of steam.

The next 20 years brought a string of dates and a lot of good times. But only once was there another real shot at a ring. Rosalyn had maintained a long-term on-again, off-again relationship with a prominent Washington, D.C. attorney. He suddenly reappeared in Rosalyn's life when she was 48, after a long absence. A whirlwind of romantic encounters followed. Rosalyn came alive with the hope that marriage was still in the offing. He had been a real ladies' man, but he was aging, too. Rosalyn thought he might be mellowing as well.

One day Rosalyn's boyfriend called her to announce a change in direction. To her astonishment, he told her that he had asked another woman to marry him.

"Why not me?" she asked Michelle and me. Pain blazed through every word. "Why couldn't it have been me that he asked?" she said.

What could we say ... that some men were dogs? What comfort would that be when it was Rosalyn's dog, a man that she'd wanted in her life? It didn't feel right to give her the "you're better off finding out now" line this time, either.

Michelle was too pissed off to say anything that might be construed as an excuse or a justification for what he had done to our friend. Hadn't Rosalyn been a good woman, a good friend, and a good lover to him? What about that prideful glow she always wore when she spoke of him and their times together? How could we forgive him for the weepy, drooping mist of betrayal and sadness he'd provoked?

We grabbed the silence and wrapped it around us like a shield. We rubbed our foreheads, trying to conjure and release some logic, some sanity, and something sensible or soothing to say. We ached for our friend, and as divorced women, we felt a little guilty about having once disposed of something she so earnestly wanted. At least we knew what we were missing. Rosalyn didn't.

We also had kids: healthy, robust, fun, and smart kids. In our dotage, there would always be someone to love us. We knew it was cold comfort to Rosalyn that her pride and joy would be a few hale and hardy mutual funds, and that her support system would be a luxury automobile to get her to appointments on time.

She had wanted a man—a particular man—and he had dogged her out in a spectacular display of unnecessary roughness, once again. It didn't matter what we thought of the guy or how we would have handled it; all that mattered was what our dear friend had wanted, for reasons that she is entitled to keep to herself. Like all of us, she deserved happiness on her terms.

But Rosalyn's traditionalism did not end at the door of domesticity. She also upheld the customary practice of black women to bounce back. The betrayal still stings—particularly when her ex-boyfriend shows up in the news, as he occasionally does in his line of work—but Rosalyn's cheerful, positive, and faithful nature is back in full force. She still dates, but not as much as she used to. Her patience is growing thin.

"I met a man who said he didn't want any drama in his life," she says.

"What did he mean by that?" I ask.

"I didn't stick around to find out. Then another man told me dating was designed to determine who's going to be in charge in the relationship. Didn't stick around for that either."

"It's not easy out there, is it?"

"No, it's so different. Men don't think they have to earn a woman's love anymore. There used to be a time when they would take three buses to come sit in your living room, hold your hand, and try their best to impress your daddy. They'd scrape together their dimes to buy you a diamond ring so small you needed three magnifying glasses to see it. But they were in love. Now, if they have any little twinge of doubt, they call it off. I've always said if you get the benefit of an exit interview with a job, why can't you have it in a relationship?"

Although many of the hopes she'd held as a young Southern girl have been dashed by the blunt realities of single life in the 21st century, Rosalyn has held on to one belief: Love may be just around the corner. "I know that I may never marry, and it's pretty much too late for me to have children. But, I still want companionship, love, and hugs," says Rosalyn. "What is it that Jesse Jackson says? Keep hope alive."

. . .

Women's spirits don't come much more vibrant than Vanessa's. It may be why she's a professional recording artist of spiritual music. Or perhaps her spirit is gentle because she's a recording artist. At any rate, Vanessa has a mellow soul.

Vanessa, 43, married when she was three months pregnant with her daughter. "I believed it was the right thing to do," she says. But the marriage didn't last long, and for the most part, Vanessa reared her child alone.

How many of us know that story? Paying the bills and keeping all the appointments, all by yourself. Being the nurse, the disciplinarian, the chauffeur, the cook, the laundress, the tutor, the event planner, and the counselor, all in one person.

Vanessa has a familiar refrain. "There were times I wanted someone to take over," she says. "I wore many hats that I didn't believe were made for my head, but I had to. I learned to be more resourceful. I'm not one to ask for help; maybe that wasn't always smart. I declined two marriage proposals. I was single by choice, and it wasn't easy."

Having come from a solid, loving two-parent family, Vanessa grew up with a much different vision of motherhood and womanhood.

"My mother was no wimp," she says. "She was intelligent, an incredible homemaker, and a master teacher. It was clear that my parents played different roles in our family, but I watched my parents do things together. I don't know if my mother ever paid bills alone, shopped alone, or went to PTA meetings alone. I doubt she ever moved furniture, pumped gasoline, or knew where to find the oil dipstick in the car. As a single mother, I had to reevaluate everything I had thought was normal."

Necessity, as we all know, is the mother of invention, and of reinvention. Vanessa learned to adapt to her life as it was, rather than as she had hoped or planned it to be.

"College was a nonnegotiable part of my daughter's future, so saving for that was a priority," she said. "I've lived modestly, clipped coupons, shopped for bargains, driven sensible cars, and chosen places to live that didn't require constant upkeep."

Like many women in similar circumstances, Vanessa sacrificed some of her own well-being and pleasure as she maintained the myriad roles she had to play as a responsible and involved single mother. She held back on dating mainly because she worried about what her young daughter would think. "I was always cautious about my daughter," Vanessa says. "I never wanted her to be able to say to me, 'You can't tell me anything,' based on what she'd seen me do. For a long time, I was uncomfortable living my own life. If I did date, I'd schedule them for the weekends my daughter spent with her father. As a teacher, I'd heard one too many my-mother's-friend stories from my female students." She says she's sure that she'd kill any boyfriend who abused her daughter.

Now that her daughter is off to college—the saving and sacrificing paid off—Vanessa has had to readjust once more. She may start dating again, but that's not a certainty.

"I know I don't take as good care of myself as I should," she says. "Perhaps when there's no one to impress, we tend to let ourselves go. Keeping fit has to be something I purposely do for myself. I'm sure that if I had seen a mental-health professional in the years following my divorce, I would have been diagnosed with depression. The failure of my family was devastating. It took longer than I care to admit to get over it, and there are still probably some lingering side effects. Maybe one of them is my choice to remain single."

For now, Vanessa is happy watching her daughter blossom into womanhood. Her music career is taking off, and she finds fulfillment in her work as an educator. She also frequently checks in on her newly widowed father, who lost a piece of his heart when Vanessa's mother died.

One relationship, she says, is already going gangbusters. Vanessa's bright disposition and conspicuous peace are rooted in her spiritual faith. When I ask her about this exclusive relationship, she says that she's been in it since the age of nine.

"How old is he?" I ask.

"Centuries," she says.

"What's his ethnicity?"

"Jewish," she says, "but many think he's a brother."

"How much education does he have?"

"He created education."

"What shall we use for his name?"

"Jesus."

This is not to say that Vanessa is ruling out mortals. She admits that she is eager—or at least somewhat eager—to meet Mr. Right. Sometimes she's inspired to take special care of her naturally good looks, just in case "he" is moving in or near her circle. Inevitably, however, she lapses into spells when she's not thinking about dating, men, or even herself. Well-meaning friends and relatives frequently prod her to get back in the game.

"They'll say, 'Look at so-and-so. He's single, has a good job, and has no kids. What's wrong with him?' Friends and family have tricked me into blind dates where we 'just happened to run into someone.' Most people assume I'm unhappy in my singleness. My age comes up often. They'll say, 'You know, you're not getting any younger,' as if I should just go outside with a sign on my back that reads, 'I'm old. Please marry me now, before I shrivel up and die.'"

The pressure comes from all corners.

"My late mother would often tell me that I needed someone to take care of me," she recalls. "I remember telling her how much I wanted to buy a house, and she told me that I should wait until I was married."

It makes Vanessa "slightly uncomfortable" to attend events where most of the attendees are couples. Like Michelle and I felt at the Jack & Jill gala, Vanessa feels like a standout—not of the diva variety, but of the sore-thumb kind.

"In spite of the movements, rallies, initiatives, laws, and supposed changes in mores, many still feel that a woman's greatest accomplishment in life is to become a wife and mother," she says. "No matter what her resumé reads, she's still looked upon with a certain degree of pity if she's not wearing a ring that a man gave her. Women I know who are in horrible relationships have implied that they're better off being stuck in their abusive situations than being alone, like their unmarried acquaintances."

She's got a demonstrable advantage over them in at least one department: "I can check the 'head-of-household' box on my 1040."

In fact, there is a lot of upside to being a single black woman these days. Vanessa's list of pluses is similar to those of many women. "I can make plans, travel, rearrange my furniture, cook or not cook, manage my finances, and make decisions without having to consult another person."

It's not as if she's wasting away or squandering her time while she's alone. Solitude can be fruitful.

"Actively pursue the thing you know in your heart that you want to do," she advises. "Use the time alone to get to know yourself. Surround yourself with people who are positively influencing your life."

Then she goes deeper.

"After my divorce, I had a difficult time reading about the virtuous woman from Proverbs. I hated her. She seemed to have so much going for her that I didn't. It took a while before I realized the key to unlocking the power of those passages in my life. The simple statement that 'she perceived her merchandise was good' was more than just an Oprah 'light-bulb moment.' It was a Fourth of July at the Washington Monument moment. This was not seeking validation, acceptance, or approval. She evaluated and accepted herself. I cannot effectively love another unless I love myself first—flaws, past, mistakes, and all. In fact, God commands my love for me! When I realized that, the hurt stopped hurting."

. . .

"Whatcha doin', Lyz?" I ask, in a sing-song voice.

"Just got out of the shower," she replies. "I worked in the yard all morning. Finally got those azaleas moved to the other side of the house."

"Oh, good for you. So you're just going to take it easy for the rest of the day?"

"Yeah. I might take a nap. I've got a date tonight."

"Ooh! With who?"

"You don't know him." No doubt she was right about that. Lyz lives in Kansas City. I haven't set foot in that town in more than a decade. I wouldn't know any of her friends or paramours. But I didn't really mean "who", anyway. I meant "what kind."

"He's this guy I used to date a long time ago," Lyz says. "He was overseas for several years and married some Italian girl, but they're divorced now, and he's back in town."

"So an old flame."

"Yes, ma'am."

"Sounds good. Is this the first date?"

"Naw. Well, it's our first real date where he's picking me up and taking me out. But I've met him for drinks and dinner a couple times."

"So maybe this is going places?"

"We'll see."

"Oh, I hope so."

"I hope so, too, but you know me. I'm fine either way. What's up with you?"

"Not a thing."

"You still aren't seeing anybody, Debbie?"

"Girl, please don't call me Debbie."

"Well, that's your name. Or a derivative of your name."

"You know I can't stand to be called Debbie. It sounds so cute and perky. I want to be provocative and sensual."

Lyz lets out one of her wild, no-holds-barred laughs and claps her hands.

"Well, you know you've still got it, girl."

"No, I don't. I said I *want* to be provocative and sensual, not that I *am*."

The laughter continues.

"Seriously, though, Deb-o-rah," Lyz says in that whiskey voice. "Nobody?"

"No-bod-ee."

"You're probably still hiding out in that house, aren't you?"

"I don't have a lick of energy left for getting all dressed up and going out. I just can't do it right now."

"You need to check yourself."

I had to get Lyz out of my business, because I'd called to get into hers. I needed her to share her secrets and lay out for me just how she came to be so cool, calm, and collected. Lyz at least seems to be the most stress-less woman I know. She has it together: Good health, good kids, good house, good job, good handle on her finances ... it's all good.

"How old are you now, Lyz?"

"52."

"Really?"

"Would I lie about that? If I were going to lie, I'd say 32."

"Okay, let me get this down. You're 52. Divorced three times, like me. Three children, like me. Flight attendant."

"Actually, I teach and train now, but you can still say flight attendant."

"You date frequently, but not regularly. Would you say that's right?"

"Hmmm. How about regularly but not frequently."

"Would you say that you have two to three dates a month?

"Something like that."

"Are each of the dates with different men?"

"That's hard to say. There can be long spells between dates with a particular guy, but he's still out there, you know?"

"In other words, he'll be back eventually."

"Usually, yeah."

What really impresses me is not the number of men Lyz sees off and on; instead, it's how she never allows any one aspect of her life to get out of hand. If she's in a relationship, she still makes plenty of time for her children (two are in college and one is still at home). She loves her work, but she uses all of her vacation time and holidays and makes a habit of being home by 6 p.m. She is a great cook and a fantastic gardener, and she insists on doing her own ironing. She's involved with a few charities (mainly through her sorority), and she sings in her church choir. In the 25 years I've known her, she has never looked unkempt, unraveled, or uncoordinated.

And the men? She's still friends with two of her exes. The third's family fawned all over Lyz at his funeral. That's how much she's got it like that.

"Tell me. What's the secret to having such a smooth-running life?"

"Rest," she says, without skipping a beat. "If you're not rested, you can't handle all the stuff there is to do, especially if you're a single mother with a job, a mortgage, tuition bills, medical bills, and so on."

"And a social life."

"A social life, and a life, period. I decided a long time ago that I wasn't going to become a martyr. 'Oh, there goes Lyz. Po' thang. She sure raised her chi'rens good, but look at her. Just pitiful.' No, thank you."

"You left some room for yourself, then."

"I did, but that takes work too. Keeping your health and your fitness takes some work. I treated it the same as my other responsibilities—the job, the kids, Little League. I scheduled it."

"That's a tight schedule."

"Very tight. But you can manage it, if you are rested."

"So how much sleep do you get?"

"About six hours a night. But I didn't say sleep. I said rest. That's not just falling in bed and passing out. It's a massage. A good book. Working in the garden. Candles around the tub. Things that relax you."

"And the men in your life—are they work or rest?"

"Oh, they're rest, baby. They've got to be. I don't allow men in my life who are projects. No, thank you. I don't need any more projects. I divorced the last project."

"So they're enhancements?"

"Precisely. That's it. Enhancements. I like that. 'Gregory, are you going to enhance my life? You're not? Then you better hit the bricks, brother!'"

There's that wild laugh again.

Lyz contends that a relaxed woman is appealing to men. "I've seen some women treat dating like it's an emergency. 'What am I going to wear? What kind of car is he driving? Is he really going to call me? Should I let him come in?' I want to say, 'Relax, baby. Just go with the flow and stop with all the stressing. He's not the last man on Earth.'"

"But you know, to some women it feels like the man they've got is the last one on Earth—especially since available black men are in such short supply."

"I know, but so what? It's always been hard for black women. What about white men sneaking into the slave quarters to get with the black women, and then selling off the black men so they wouldn't be competition? The supply problem isn't anything new."

"You should see the statistics, Lyz. Something like 40 percent of black women have never been married. I know marriage isn't for everybody, but most women at least want a man they could marry if they wanted to."

"Then they need to relax," she says. "Reee-lax. Just be who you are. What dress would you wear if you were going out by yourself or with your girlfriends or your father? That's the dress you should wear on a date."

"You're telling me you've never bought a new outfit for a date, or put a lot of thought into what you were going to wear?"

"I have, but I realized how stupid I was. I can't stand putting on airs, because you're either going to have to fake like that forever if you end up with him, or you're going to have to break down and be yourself."

"All right, Miss Expert on Marriage."

"I am an expert. I'm damn sure an expert on what goes wrong in marriage. I think a lot of it comes from being fake. You may not be doing it for bad reasons, but it doesn't matter. When the jig is up, there's trouble."

"People do change, Lyz."

"Change is fine. Some change is natural. I'm not saying that when you stop having sex four or five times a day, you've been exposed as a fake. Those are habits. I'm talking about personality, character, and the real self. Don't dress it up and don't dress it down. Some women play dumb or helpless, you know. Just be you."

There's silence for a moment as I try to capture every one of Lyz's words.

"Look," she says. "Can we finish this sometime later? I've got to take a nap."

"I just have a few more questions," I beg.

"If you don't mind, let's talk later," she pushes.

"Okay, fine," I pout. "You need your rest for the big date."

"Got to have the rest, sweetie," she says. "You ought to try it sometime."

. . .

For practically all of her adult life, Cecelia has done it all—wife, mother of two, a time as a stay-at-home mom, and a time as a career woman. In 2002, however, Cecilia's marriage to her college sweetheart ended after 24 years. It didn't end for any particular reason, but instead for scores of little ones that chip away at the love, trust, and hope that preserve a relationship.

Cecilia didn't do much socially in the first two years after her divorce. Taking care of her daughters, working, running a household, and making ends meet were enough. Any spare time she had went to decompressing from her various challenges and mounting tensions.

She also had to nurse her daughters through the transition. Her youngest daughter took it particularly hard, since she was still too young to understand why marriages come undone. Soon afterward, her older daughter had a baby while still living at home, so she had yet another big adjustment. Divorcée, head of household, and grandmother are a lot of titles to take on in the span of two years.

By her third year as a single woman, Cecilia has wrestled her new routines into submission. She finally felt sturdy enough to reenter the dating world for the first time in nearly three decades, but a lot had changed over the years, as Cecilia quickly realized.

She first noticed that women outnumbered men everywhere she went, and the air of competition was thicker than she'd remembered. She found herself disappointed with the quality of conversations she had with men, but she figured that they didn't need to use any skills to keep a woman's interest anymore ... or at least they *thought* they didn't. After all, the law of supply and demand was on their side.

"One man told me he could never have a relationship because he wanted a dumb woman. He said dumb women are hassle-free and sub-missive," Cecilia says. "I appreciated that. Honesty matters most."

After a few more demoralizing encounters, Cecilia packed it in. She had tested the waters of the single scene and found them to be uncomfortable and possibly even dangerous. She became a Shrinker and took a pass on any activity that wasn't absolutely necessary.

However, Cecilia's high-energy, effervescent personality wasn't cut out for such a low-key lifestyle, so she began a rather intensive campaign of self-improvement that included regular visits to muse-ums, trips to the theater, a gym membership, and a real-estate course. Soon, she became a Coaster.

"I would love to have a man who adores me. I would love to feel that excitement, but it has to be right," Cecilia says confidently. "Now that I've discovered the real me from the inside out, rather than the outside in, I'm willing, ready, and capable of entering a relationship. But there must be a spiritual connection, the communication must be effective, and there must be mutual respect."

In fact, Cecilia is so comfortable with her life now that I wondered if a man would be help or a hindrance.

"This may sound harsh, but what's a man good for, as far as you're concerned?" I ask.

"Entertainment. Emotional support," she says. "For me, that is. I can work, and I can feed myself. I can do all the survival-in-the-wilderness stuff. But when I come home from the wilderness, it would be nice to have someone say, 'Hey, I see you've had a rough day. Let's have a bubble bath and some wine.' I don't want someone who would be threatened or intimidated, or who would try to put me in a box. That's too much drama."

Like other Coasters, Cecilia is a philosopher who pays a lot of attention to her feelings. Doing so has helped her put things into context and sort out what matters.

"The main thing I'm looking for is willingness," she said. "A man may or may not know how to effectively communicate, but he must want to try. That's okay with me. If that's the case, I'm willing to share. If he's stuck, not willing, or mean, it won't work."

· 8 ·

Double Dippers

Marva and norene are not true Sole Sisters. They are former Sole Sisters, and may be again some day, but neither qualifies for the title now. Both of them are married, and they only act like single women.

. . .

I met Marva in one of Istanbul's ubiquitous corner stores. She was trying to get directions from a native who only spoke a few words of English. When you're an American living in Turkey—especially a black American—you pay attention when you hear a familiar language and a familiar accent, and you really perk up when you see that the voice accompanies a fellow black face.

"You're American," I said, smiling at Marva.

"Oh, my goodness, you are too!" she said, delighted and relieved. We hugged each other like old friends. "I can't tell you how glad I am to see you," Marva said, and then launched into a recitation of two difficult days in the old city.

Within five minutes, I learned that Marva was from Florida, that she had just turned 60, that she was married to an older businessman who was white, and that she had come to Turkey for a conference on world hunger. Also within that brief span of time, she showed me a stack of pictures that she carried with her always. There was one of her with President Clinton; one of her with Vice President Al Gore;

one of her with some Florida state officials; and one of her with her husband. She was proudest, however, of a photo of her with a handsome, middle-aged man in a military uniform.

"This is my Turkish boyfriend," she said. "I met him back home; he was working with NATO command. He's amazing … so sophisticated and brilliant! He treated me like a queen, girl. He always told me I was his queen. We went places and he bought me some beautiful things. I really like him a lot."

Technically, we were still strangers. But she opened that door, so I stepped in. "Is he here now or still in Florida?" I asked.

"Oh, he's in Ankara, which is his home base. He's married, though." Our eyes met. "That's a problem," she said.

"Yeah, I guess so," I replied. "Are you trying to see him?"

"I'm supposed to, but he became really nervous when I called and told him I was here. He told me he would call me today or tomorrow about getting together. Either I'll go there or he'll come here. He'll call."

I had an appointment to keep and had to leave this intriguing woman, but we traded cell phone numbers and promised to get together later.

For the next week, Marva and I spent some part of every day together. We shopped in the bazaar, and we shared lunch and tea twice and dinner once. One afternoon, we sat in the lobby of my apartment building and talked. On each occasion, our discussions invariably returned to the Turkish air force officer.

"Have you heard from him?"

"He didn't call me. So I called him. I think he's giving me the runaround, and I told him so. I told him I didn't appreciate him promising to see me and then not being available. I think he's worried about his wife finding out, but I'll bet she already suspects something. She answered the phone when I called."

"She did?"

"Yeah. I didn't say anything about us, but he was probably acting nervous about it. Women know these things, you know."

Marva, who is tall and has a girlish figure, cuts a stunning pose.

She knows she doesn't look 60. Every time I saw her—no matter how early or late it might have been—she was completely put-together. Her makeup, jewelry, and clothes suggested she was going out on the town. As we chatted one afternoon in my apartment building's lobby, Marva mentioned that she needed to go souvenir shopping for her grandchildren. On the spur of the moment, we decided to walk a few blocks over to Taksim Square, a popular landmark known for a variety of shops, restaurants, and theaters. Marva was wearing black slacks, a satiny blouse set off with a glittery brooch, and dangling earrings. Her long auburn hair was perfectly in place. I was wearing a denim skirt, a nondescript cotton top, and flip-flops—ideal garb, in my opinion, for a visit to a bustling, casual district in the middle of a muggy Turkish summer.

Apparently, Marva wouldn't be caught dead dressed like that in public, and apparently, she didn't think I would either. "I'll wait here while you go up and change," she said. When I told her I was going as I was, she said "Oh," in a half-shocked, half-disapproving way. Off we went—two new friends thrown together by chance. We were bound by nationality, by ethnicity, by gender, and by suspense over Marva's unusual, and convoluted, love affair.

Something of a social butterfly back home in Florida, Marva had met the Turkish officer—a lieutenant colonel—at a reception at the local air base. She was accustomed to meeting interesting people there and since she was naturally coquettish, she often enjoyed harmless flirtations with some of them. However, this man was different. Marva was surprised that she was immediately attracted by his uniform, bronze complexion, accent, and debonair style. "He's so sexy," she gushed, even after he'd stood her up. She pulled that photo out again. "Look at him. Isn't he sexy? This was taken not long after we met."

"How did you become lovers?"

"Well, first of all, I don't believe in infidelity, okay? I consider my-self to be very honest and responsible. But my husband is an alcoholic. He has a real problem, and he doesn't want to do anything about it. I haven't had sex with him in a long time. We just live together." She also said that her husband had become "funny" about his money. "He has a lot of money, but his family doesn't want him to spend any of it on me. Something's up there."

Marva wasn't proud of caving in to temptation. "But I've asked God to forgive me for it, and He has," she said confidently. "I'm still a healthy, normal woman, and my needs weren't being met anymore. I'm a good woman, and I know I deserve a good man. I offered to show him around since he didn't know anybody in the States, and it wasn't long at all before he started coming on to me. I was really attracted to him. Like I said before, he treated me like a queen. One night, we just couldn't take it anymore, and we made love."

I swear that I'm not making up the next part.

Upon her arrival in Istanbul, Marva discovered that one of her pieces of luggage was missing. When the airline delivered it to her hotel the next day, she noticed a strip of tape around the suitcase that indicated the baggage had been searched by hand. "The only thing I could think of that would provoke them to hand-search the bag was this little film canister I had in there. You see, I kept the sheet that was on the bed the night we made love as a … as a memento, I guess. I cut out a piece of the spot that was wet and put it in the canister and brought it with me. That's how much it meant to me. I guess with all the 9/11 business, they thought I had some kind of biological weapon or something." She laughed. "I guess it is biological, but it's not a weapon!"

That's how lovestruck Marva was.

Eventually, my intriguing American friend stopped trying to reach her runaway lover. She turned her attentions to a small recording studio on the Asian side of the ancient city, hoping to make some connection with the music community. Upon her return to Florida, Marva called to say that she had performed with the house bands at a couple of nightspots in Istanbul. She was already planning a return visit, but she said she'd never heard from the colonel.

Meanwhile, Marva says she isn't sure what she's going to do about her marriage, which is as unsatisfactory as ever. She talks about the kind of man she wants in her life as if the demise of her current union is a foregone conclusion. He's got to be mature and intelligent, she says. And, she adds, he has to have money, because she likes nice things and wants to travel internationally. "I'm not paying for it. I'm not giving my money to any man," she says.

Marva also wants to write a book about her life. She's got the material, that's for sure.

· · ·

Considering the genre—married women who double as singles—Norene has a more ordinary story. She lives with Stan, her husband of 31 years, in a roomy split level in northern Mississippi. Their three children—two daughters and a son—live outside the state.

Norene and Stan still make appearances as a couple. They go to church together, show up at weddings and funerals together, and even grocery shop together. But they haven't shared a bed, or a bedroom, since 1997, the year the last child left home.

"If it hadn't been for the kids being at home, it would have been before then," Norene says. "We slept in the same bed, but that's all we did, sleep. We just lost our feelings for one another. I think we got married too young and just grew in different ways."

I ask Norene if hers was a case of staying together for the children's sake.

"Absolutely," she says.

"Then may I ask why you're still together now since the kids are grown and gone?"

"Because at this point, it doesn't make sense to separate. What difference would it make? All it would be is a bunch of hassle and expense. We don't need that. He does his thing, and I do mine."

"What does your 'thing' involve?"

"Doing what I want to do, when I want and with whomever I want."

"Going out?"

"If that's what I want to do, yes. I go to Memphis a lot, usually with a friend of mine. Stan goes to Tunica with his buddies a lot to drink and gamble and who knows what else."

"Do you think he's fooling around?"

"I'm sure he is. At least some of the time."

"And that doesn't bother you?"

"Not one tiny bit. See, I don't have those feelings for him, so I don't care. I don't have to worry about him bringing anything home to me, because we don't get together anymore. So if that's what he wants to do …"

"And what about you?" I ask.

"I've got my ways," Norene says, teasingly. "There's a guy in Memphis."

Richard is Norene's "guy" in the river city. He's 54, divorced, and for a long time, he lived with a woman in what Norene calls "a common-law situation." Richard still has ties to his former live-in love. To hear Norene tell it, the woman "bugs him about money constantly," and she's "half crazy." Richard usually capitulates to the woman's demands, according to Norene, "because he's an easy-going guy, so he just gives her the money to shut her up. But, sooner or later, she'll be back."

Norene doesn't know if Stan knows or even suspects what his wife is doing on her frequent junkets to Memphis. She's fairly sure that he doesn't care. "Stan isn't going to say anything even if he does think something's going on. I told you, we're not like married people. We have what I guess you would call an arrangement."

"What does Richard think about all this?"

"He wants me to move to Memphis, but I'm not doing that. My job is here. I could probably get a job in Memphis, but I've got seniority where I am, and I like the way things are going. I'm probably going to move into a supervisor's position next year. I'm not about to throw that away and start over."

"Would he consider moving to where you are?"

"I hope not! That would be a lot of mess I don't need. I've already got a husband. I don't need that. I think Stan might get mad, because sooner or later people would find out, and Stan would be embar-rassed ... not to mention my kids. I'm not going to rub his face in it." Norene said she has told Richard to stay put, and that she'll continue coming to him for the occasional rendezvous.

"I know you must think I'm crazy," Norene said. "Believe me, this is not what I thought was going to happen. I don't feel great about it, but I don't feel bad about it either. Stan and I are used to each other. We get along fine, and we stay out of each other's way. I'm in my prime, and if I can have a nice time with a man and not hurt anybody, I don't see what's wrong with that. It would be different if Stan still had feelings for me, but he doesn't. So ..." Her voice drifts off.

"Where's this going, Norene?"

"With me and Stan, or with me and Richard?"

"Both."

"As far as I can tell, Stan and me are fine with they way things are. We have this understanding. But Richard? I guess it will just go on like it is now until something happens."

Flamekeepers

THERE IS ONE TYPE OF SINGLE BLACK WOMAN that stands alone: the widow. Today, nearly 1.5 million black women are widows, and Carla became one of them in 1995.

. . .

Carla and James had been married for 30 years. When leaving the house for work one April day, James doubled over with pain. The heart attack was his second. The first, which had happened more than eight years before, had been mild but frightening. This one was fatal. James was pronounced dead on arrival at the hospital.

"Something in me just knew that was it," Carla says. "With the first one, he called me from the service station up the street and said, 'Honey, come and get me, I think I'm having a heart attack.' But this time, it was like he couldn't get a word out. When I finally got him to look at me, I could see it in his eyes ..."

Carla bites her lip. Tears well in her eyes. "It still gets me," she says in a whisper. "It was his goodbye to me. It flashes in my mind all the time."

"You really loved each other, didn't you?"

"Yes," she says, sniffing. "We really did. We had been together a long time, you know. After all that time, you get addicted to a person, to all of his habits and his ways of doing things. We were pretty happy together."

"Was he your first love?"

"I thought I was in love with another man before him, a boy I grew up with named Wilfred. He went into the service as soon as he turned 18, and when he came home, he'd changed and didn't seem interested in me the same way. Then he moved away. I guess he was my first love."

"When did you meet James?"

"August of 1963. We were both at Howard University. He was a sophomore and I was a scared-as-heck freshman."

"What was it about him that attracted you?"

"His upbeat attitude. He was a good-looking young man, and so clean. He was real easy on the eyes. But his personality was the key to his charm. He treated you like he was so comfortable with you. Everybody loved James."

"When did you get married?"

"June 26, 1965—back when girls got married young. I was 20, and James was going to be a senior. We could have waited, but we didn't want to. We'd started acting like we were married—we started having sex—and I didn't feel right about that. I'm an old-fashioned country girl. I told him, 'If we're going to keep doing this, we have to make it right.' He didn't hesitate, so I called my mama, and we planned a wedding."

"You and James had four children?"

"Three girls and a boy. They've all got their own families now. Dionna just got married about two years ago, and she and her husband are expecting their first baby now. They live near Richmond, Virginia. He's a coach and she teaches music. All of the others are scattered around the country, but I see them about once or twice a year. I have four children, four grandchildren, and another grandchild on the way."

"Dionna keeps you company, no doubt."

"Oh yes. She's a good babysitter to her old and tired mom."

"What do you mean, 'old and tired.'"

"Just what I said."

"Do you ever date? Do you ever see anyone?"

Carla shifts in her chair, rests her chin in her hand and slowly shakes her head.

"I've had opportunities, but I turned them down. I just can't make myself do it."

"Why not?"

She leans back in the chair, lets out a sigh, and stares at the ceiling. Carla bites her lip again, but says nothing. After a long pause, she leans forward and speaks, her voice low and soft.

"Deborah, when you have spent 30-plus years of your life with a man and he's been all you know for all that time, you don't even know how to think of yourself with someone else. I wouldn't know how to begin dating again. You know how different everything is now? What would I look like out there trying to date?"

"You'd look like a beautiful woman who is still alive and still has some living to do."

"I'd look like a pitiful woman who's looking for someone to take care of me."

"No, you wouldn't, Carla."

"And I'm so naïve. I wouldn't know how to talk to a man. He could use me and trick me, feed me a bunch of bull that sounds good, and I'd just say, 'Oh, really? Wow, really?' If a man tried to kiss me? Honey, I would just faint."

"Maybe you'll consider it sometime later."

"I doubt it. I've thought about this. Like I said, I've had opportunities. There are some very nice men who would like to take me out. But I'm not ready for this, and I might not ever be ready."

"Because of James?"

"Because of James, and because of my children and grandchildren. I don't want them to have to worry about me or wonder even for a second if I've forgotten about their daddy because I haven't, and I never will. He will always be my heart."

"Obviously, remarriage is out of the question for now."

"For now and forever. I was married for 30 years to James, and that was my marriage. I don't want to be someone else's wife, and if I do go out with someone, he's going to have to understand that if James could walk back through that door again, he'd be history. I know people say 'never say never,' but there are some things you just know."

"But you won't say 'never' to dating?"

"I'll say 'almost never.' Does that work?"

. . .

You'll never mistake Bobbi for the proverbial "little ol' lady from Pasadena." She moved there 15 years ago after her husband, Franklin, succumbed to pancreatic cancer. Instead of retiring, though, Bobbi found a new lease on life in her adopted city.

"My daughter and my sister say I am never still," she says in rapid-fire cadence. "I keep moving. I'm doing something all the time. It's really important to feeling good and youthful. So is sex. You have to keep having sex, because if you don't, you get old, and then you get fat."

This admonition comes from a woman creeping up on her 70th birthday, though Bobbi neither looks it nor, to hear her tell it, feels it.

"When someone is bold or foolish enough to ask me how old I am, I tell them, 'Old enough to know what I'm doing.' What difference does my age make? I firmly believe that you're as young as you feel, and I feel like I'm 30 most of the time. Naturally, it takes some effort to keep yourself up when you get to be my number—that's what I call my age, my 'number'. I get a facial every week, I keep my nails up, and now my sister and I meditate."

"And is she widowed or married?"

"Ella's divorced."

"Oh, so it's just the two of you sisters having a good time."

"Ella has a boyfriend—a regular fella. I don't have one particular man, but I go out a lot."

"And how are these men?"

"They're great. Most of them are widowers, but one or two, I think, are divorced men."

"How many are there?"

"Just three. I could see more than that if I wanted to. I get flirted with a lot. But a man has to be friends with me first. Some are romantic partners, but there's only one that I have relations with. He keeps me young."

"Does he have a problem with you seeing other men?"

"I wouldn't care if he did, and if he does, he'll be smart to keep it to himself. I'm way past the stage of anyone telling me what to do. My daughter doesn't try to, and my sister doesn't try to. Franklin didn't even try to. There's no way I'm going to put up with that from anyone else."

"But he does know that you're not having sex with anyone else, right?"

"I think he assumes that. And he's right if he does assume that. He knows that I have class. He's always saying that I'm classy."

After Franklin died, two years passed before Bobbi would even entertain the idea of seeing other men. She buried herself in her work—she ran a cosmetology school in Louisiana—and kept busy during the days as chairwoman of her church's missionary society and in the evenings with her bridge club. When her sister got a divorce, she and Bobbi decided to start over. Bobbi sold her house, cashed out of her business, and headed for the California hills.

"You wouldn't believe how quickly I adjusted," she says. "This was a whole different place for me, but when I said I was going to start over, I really meant it. Ella had been a housewife, so it was a big change for her too. But we started a consignment shop with another woman out here—she's divorced—and things started just clicking."

"And it was in Pasadena that you started dating?"

"Well, I guess you could say I had one or two dates back home. But they didn't amount to anything. Plus, everybody knew me there and the tongues were wagging so much. They had me going out with men I didn't even know. I wasn't really interested in any of those fellas."

"You didn't have any of those hang-ups that some widows have?"

"You mean about seeing other men?"

"Yes."

"Oh, no. Not even a doubt. Franklin and I believed in enjoying ourselves. Would he have just dried up if I had died first? Nope. You can ask Ella. Up until the day he got really sick, he was trying to have a good time. I don't feel like I'm betraying him in the least bit. I'm just trying to enjoy my life as long as I can. And I am."

. . .

Pauline is as retiring and shy as Bobbi is active and outgoing. A widow since 1989, she lives alone in a mid-sized Southern city. Her two grown sons, who live in the same city, come over often to take care of her lawn and other responsibilities around the house. They have been pleading with Pauline to move in with them ever since her husband, Ernest, died from injuries in a traffic accident in Oklahoma.

"I might go live with them in a few years," she says. "But right now, I'm fine where I am with all my things, and I don't want to be in the way. They've got their own families, and their own lives, and I can still take good care of myself. I'll move in with them when I can't do things for myself as well."

Ernest's sudden death left Pauline understandably stunned. She was also unprepared. "I didn't know how to do things like paying bills," she said. "That's one thing I would say to women: Know how to manage things, because you never know. There are some things I'm still learning, and Ernie's been gone quite some time now. I even told my daughter-in-law that she'd better learn how to do things. Of course, she's married to my son, and I don't want anything to happen to him, but you just never know. Ernie was with the railroad, and the benefits are so good that I didn't have to start working again. I've got high blood pressure, so I stopped working a long time ago … about five years before my husband passed."

"What about a social life?" I ask.

"A what?"

"What do you do for pleasure or for fun or relaxation?"

The question makes Pauline cackle.

"A social life, hmmm," she says, twisting her mouth. "Well, let's see, I go to church a lot. I'm there several times a week for one thing or another. Once in a while I go to a movie, but they cost a lot now, so I kinda cut back on that. Other than that, I go to my children's houses or my friend Joanne's house. She's a real smart lady who used to be a school principal. She's a widow like me, but her husband died about two years ago."

"What about going out with men?"

"I don't go out with men," Pauline says emphatically. "You sound like Joanne. She's always after me about going out and courting someone. Connie—that's my daughter-in-law—she says the same thing. Like I tell them, I'll tell you: Don't talk to me about men."

I was inclined to honor Pauline's request, but apparently I'd touched a nerve. After pouting for a moment, she started up again.

"One time I went to lunch with this man from church. It was after the service, and he asked me if he could buy me Sunday dinner. Well, I must have been feeling kinda sassy, because I said all right, and we went to this nice little place down the river. The food was pretty good."

"And the company?"

"The company was all right. He was real polite and all. I think a lot of the single women—the older single women—at the church have their eye on him, so I guess they call him kind of a catch. I was just looking at him as a nice man. We had a nice talk, and it was all right. When he took me back to get my car in the parking lot at church, he tried to hold my hand, and that just made me feel kind of cheap, or dirty, or something. I didn't like it. My friend says that's stupid, but I can't help it. 'Specially not there on the church grounds."

"You think it would have been different if it had been somewhere else?"

"No, I don't think so. I just think I'm the type that gets married one time in her life, and that's who she's with from then on."

"But don't the marriage vows say 'til death'?"

"That's what the marriage vows say, but I still don't feel right being with anybody else."

"It was just hand-holding."

"Hand-holding for now, but then a kiss on the cheek, then a kiss on the lips. I'm not trying to be prudish or anything. It's fine for women when their husbands are gone, and they still have time to live. But it's not right for me. I don't need to experiment with it either. I know it's not right for me."

. . .

Some Sole Sisters are just biding their time. They've got the man they want all to themselves. They've got no need for singles bars or singles clubs or singles cruises or dating services or matchmaking videos.

These women are committed to monogamous relationships. Some live separately from their mates. Some live with them. At one time in their lives, they may have been keenly aware of the paucity of men. But it's somebody else's problem now. For them, the deal is done. The search is over. They are single in name only.

· 10 ·

Knitters

Everyday after work, Crystal goes home and puts something in the microwave to defrost. In about an hour, she'll start dinner for Brandon and herself … some kind of chicken dish, usually. The apartment they share is tidy, but small: One bedroom, one bathroom, a tight kitchen with a small dining nook, and a living room that eats up too much square footage.

It was Brandon's apartment first. After they'd been together for four months, Crystal decided it was ridiculous to keep all of her belongings in her apartment when all of her was always at Brandon's. So, she moved in about two years ago.

"I only have a part-time job, so I do all of the house stuff," Crystal says. "I don't mind doing it all. But when I go to work full-time, that's going to change. We've already talked about it. He knows he's going to have to do some things."

"What does he do now when he gets home?" I ask.

"He crashes," she says. "He goes straight to the shower and then right to the couch. He sleeps until dinner."

"What kind of work does he do?"

"He's on a highway crew," she says. "So he's really worn out. He's not lazy or anything."

"Do you all go out anymore?"

"Every now and then," says Crystal, sounding a little ashamed. "We used to be in the streets all the time. But we've cooled out some. It was too expensive."

"Do you miss it?"

"Not really. I guess a little. Sometimes. I miss being with my friends."

"When's the last time you saw them?"

"Like, out?"

"Yeah."

"Brandon and I went out with them about 10 days ago. There was a rehearsal dinner for a couple we know, and they had an after-party when all of the parents and grandparents had gone home. Brandon and I had a blast."

"Since then?"

"We haven't been anywhere since then. Just work and the grocery store."

"May I ask you about your love life?"

"Oh, it's still good. I'd say better because now we are so comfortable with each other."

"Where do you see this going? What happens next?"

"We'll probably get married. We haven't really talked about it, but there's kind of an understanding that we will."

"What do you think will make that come to pass?"

"Probably getting more financially secure. If he gets another promotion, I think he will feel better about it."

Crystal and Brandon are both 25. She says he's partied out and ready to settle down, and that he likes the stability of a one-to-one relationship. However, she sounds a little tentative about her own desires.

"I feel a lot older than my friends. They don't call me or come over much. I think they think they're disturbing us. But Brandon wouldn't mind at all, and I sure wouldn't mind. But they would probably try to get me to go out somewhere too."

"That wouldn't be a problem, would it?"

"No. Brandon isn't jealous or possessive like that. He trusts me, like I trust him."

"Then why don't you do it every now and then just to see your girls?"

"Because once I'm out there, I really don't feel right. It's fun to be with those crazy people, but there's really nothing out there for me. I don't feel right dancing with some strange guy or getting hit on by dudes in the clubs. When you say no, they get mad, and my friends always tell me to go on, go on. It's just too much drama."

"It sounds like you've got your reasons."

"I do. But I don't want to lose all my friends."

"Since you like to cook, why don't you just have a bunch of them over for dinner?"

"I might do that sometime. That's a good idea. But, I don't want to sound like I'm complaining or anything. Those girls may look like they're having a good time, but all they're trying to do is get where I already am. I'm really glad I'm with Brandon. I like the way we're living right now. We could use more room and more money, but we're doing pretty well. I'm happy. I am."

. . .

Faith met Michael in first grade. During their elementary school years, they conducted a kiddie courtship. When they reached junior high, Michael's family moved to Texas, but a dozen years later, Faith and Michael reconnected by chance.

"I went to visit a college classmate. One night, we went to a party, and who was there but Michael. I couldn't believe it … after all those years. We started talking, reminiscing, and catching up, and I remember thinking how cute he was. He was the same funny, easygoing Mike, but he was fine, too."

An adult version of their long-ago courtship ensued. The distance between their home cities—Faith was living in Maryland—meant a commuter relationship. They took turns flying back and forth to see one another. The long absences helped keep the courtship fresh and added a tinge of adventure, but it was costly and, on some nights, frustrating.

Fed up with her job and the long-distance courtship, Faith talked it over with her sister, mother, and brother, and then quit her job and headed to the Lone Star State.

"It was so exciting we could hardly stand it. Actually seeing each other every day … that was fantastic," she says.

Then Faith and Michael hit a rough patch. This was his town, and he'd spent half of his life there. He had friends, favorite haunts, and a routine. Now, Faith was there, and she wanted Michael's undivided attention.

"I'll confess I wanted him just to smother me once I moved to Texas," she says. "I thought that was the plan. If we *could* be together, then we *would*. Of course, I did see him a lot. But not all the time, like I expected."

The tensions caused by conflicting expectations began to worsen and, soon, Faith and Michael were trapped in a cycle of fighting and making up. Michael responded by being around even less. When Faith confronted him, Michael protested that she was trying to control him.

"Finally, we had a serious talk," she explains. "Really serious. It went on for hours, and then days. We had to admit that the change in our situation wasn't a panacea, and that it didn't make things perfect. We had to adjust to being around one another all the time. I hadn't thought about that. But that's what was happening. Thank God we were able to work it out. We really do love each other."

Before she and Michael reconnected, Faith had been a self-avowed workaholic. "No man, no distractions from work," she says. "Working all the time helped the time pass by without me thinking about not having a man in my life. I don't believe for a second that every woman has to have somebody, but I really want to be a mother. I wouldn't have children without being married first. I was still young but as more and more birthdays came and went, I began to get worried. I'm really big on planning, and my plan was to take my time getting to know my potential husband—really getting to know him—and then, after marriage, taking a few years to get accustomed to that. Then the children would come. So that's why age 25 wasn't really as young as it seemed."

The dating scene annoyed her. "So many of our black men are either in prison or just not together that it makes it tough to find a mate," she says. "And the men that are successful? I have found them to be so superficial, which is a big turn-off. They want you to praise them for not having been in jail!"

She did like the freedom of singlehood. "No checking in, and no disappointment," she says. "It's great for a while. In fact, I think all women need that. But then you get to the point where you want to be with someone."

Faith has more education than Michael, and she makes more money than he does. She thinks that had something to do with the early tensions too. But when you see them together, you think of a long-married couple. They finish each other's sentences, they have lots of inside jokes, each picks up the other's nuances, and there's a feeling that each is always at least aware of, if not always in tune with, the other's moods and needs.

"Things are going well. Michael is really wonderful. He's not perfect, but nobody's perfect. For sure, I'm not. I think that's part of the maturing process, to get it straight in your head what's important. Some things can't be compromised, or shouldn't be, in my opinion, as that's only delaying the inevitable. Some people are miserable and just staying together for the heck of it. I had to realize that I'm not going to get Mr. Perfect in Michael, and he's not going to get Miss Perfect in me. But he has all the qualities that really matter to me. He's God-loving, adores his family, is comfortable with himself, is supportive, and has a great sense of humor."

Marriage is a foregone conclusion for Faith and Michael. They don't live together and won't, she says. "I want that to be a new experience when we do get married," says Faith. For now, she still shares an apartment with her younger sister, a college student who also made the move to Texas, and Michael lives alone across town. Her work as a pharmaceutical sales representative feeds her workaholic tendencies. Michael still nurtures his "inner homeboy" with occasional all-male outings. But the two are beginning to master the give-and-take, the balancing act that a strong, healthy relationship requires.

"My advice for single black women who want a relationship is to pray and believe that God hears you," says Faith. "My story with

Michael is evidence of God answering prayer. And if I found love, trust me, everyone can."

. . .

Zena has a common beef about being a single black woman. Since she has no husband or children, her employer assumes she doesn't mind working long hours or nights, weekends, and holidays. Even some of her relatives "rely on me to do everything," thinking she has all the time in the world, and perhaps even thinking that their demands make her feel needed. At the same time, her intimates keep bugging her about her single status. "They usually mention that my eggs will be drying up, so I should hurry up and have children," says Zena, 32.

She expects they'll back off once she marries Remy, the 38-year-old telecommunications specialist she's been seeing exclusively for five years and with whom she lives in Maryland. They've been talking about it.

"I love the family unit and I want to have kids in a two-parent house," says Zena, a television producer. "And I do not want to grow old alone."

When she was on the singles circuit, Zena—a long-haired, brown-skinned beauty—was routinely disappointed by the way men looked at her once they discovered she had a college degree and an exciting job. "The modern-day black woman is so independent and self-sufficient," she says. "Many black men feel intimidated and awkward with a woman who doesn't need a man but longs for or wants one. People are wrong if they think all single black women are too bull-headed, independent, and unwilling to share their world. Black men are a wonderful species—complicated, but unique and loving, and I wouldn't trade them for anything. But they do come with complications, and it requires patience and understanding and hope. There are men out there who do have it together, but you have to be diligent in your search, pray, and remember that we all have frailties."

If Zena had her druthers, Remy would be a better listener. A higher tax bracket would be a plus too. But as she says, no one's perfect. She's happy enough with Remy's other qualities—a man who notices her; a man who is "gentle and caring, yet tough when the occasion calls for it." To Zena, he is a Christian man with a goal.

. . .

They don't have children together, but they do share an address, a mortgage, two dogs, and a time-share in Daytona Beach. Belinda and Al are as good as married, but they have no contract. When they first moved in together more than a dozen years ago, they thought about getting married. Alfred bought an engagement ring, and Belinda wore it. But, when they announced their intentions to relatives and everyone started arguing about all those *musts*—where they *must* hold the ceremony, who *must* perform the ritual, who *must* be on the guest list—Belinda and Al decided to elope. But they could never find a time that worked, and the talk of elopement, and then the talk of marriage, slowed to a halt. Today, Belinda still wears the ring.

"Without ever saying so, we agreed to drop the whole thing," Belinda explains. "At some point, Al asked me how badly I wanted to be married, and I was offended by the question because it implied that the marriage was just for me. So I said something to the effect of, 'I don't have to be married; I'm fine the way I am.' I think that may have been the last time we really addressed the subject. I was being stubborn at first, but now, I think we accidentally made the right decision."

Still, everybody thinks they're married. In fact, Belinda says everybody treats them like a long-married couple. "He's always called my husband, and I seldom bother to correct them. We are about as married as you can get, except that we don't have a piece of paper on file that recognizes us a married couple. At the end of the day, it's not something we need."

"Are there any downsides to a quasi-marriage?" I ask.

"If we had children, I think that would have been unfair to them," she says. "So that just never happened."

As much as she loves Al, and as much as she insists she never has doubted her commitment to him, Belinda does not think they will ever make their union "official."

"We don't see how it would help anything," she said. "Our relationship is more solid than any legal marriage I know of. We're solid as a rock, like Ashford & Simpson sing. And who knows? Getting married might hurt the relationship."

"How so?"

"I don't know. I don't know that it would. But, as they say, why fix it if it ain't broke? We just don't want to tamper with a good thing. After all this time, we still really do have a good thing."

· 11 ·

Trippers

A s we've seen, even those Sole Sisters who are aching for companionship are often thriving otherwise. They've put their circumstances in perspective—shoved them there, in some cases—and on the whole live fairly complete lives. Few fall apart for want of a man; it's not the sister way. Black women are amazingly resilient, which partially explains the surge in educational accomplishments, career advancements, high incomes, and home ownership among single black women. Regardless of our Sole Sister types, we aren't generally inclined to put our dreams and ambitions on hold until Mr. Right happens along.

But there are some Sole Sisters who are hostages to a fantasy. They live in suspended animation, waiting for the proverbial knight on the white horse to rescue them from destitution, loneliness, or hopelessness, and they often fail to see themselves for what they really are—bereft of self-esteem. Trippers are the shame of the Sole Sisterhood.

. . .

Don't ask me why Katrina is still with Jamal. Their relationship sounds like a trip down whitewater rapids with neither a paddle nor a boat. By her own admission, Katrina is miserable, but she doesn't even have to say it. She wears her misery in her eyes, her body language, and her voice.

"We have a baby together, so that's one reason," she says. "At least he takes care of our son. He plays with him, and takes him places sometimes. He's okay as a father. The baby has everything he needs; at least I can give him that."

Katrina's baby boy was born at the same time another young woman was pregnant by Jamal. She found out about the other woman shortly before she gave birth.

"I had heard he was messing around with this girl, but I didn't know it was as bad as that," she says.

"Shouldn't it have been enough that he was cheating, Katrina?" I ask, concerned about her situational ethics.

"Yeah, it should have. But having a baby with someone else? That really hurt me. I might have been able to get over it if it were just sex. Men don't shock me when they have sex with more than one woman at a time. But it did shock me that the girl was pregnant by Jamal."

"Does he take care of that baby too?"

"Financially, yeah. Not as much as he does for our baby, but he gives her some money every month. At least that's what he tells me."

"Does he spend time with his other child?"

"I don't think so. He showed me a picture of him holding her when she was a few days old, but I'm not sure he's seen her since then."

"How does that make you feel?"

"He's that baby's daddy, and he has to take responsibility for that. But it's not like they're a family or anything like that. So, no, it wouldn't work for him to be going over there, spending time with the little girl and probably her mother, too, and at the same time trying to be a family with me and our son."

"So you feel like a family?"

"We are a family."

"Any talk of getting married someday?"

Katrina blushes. "One of these days," she says, slowly, and with a giggle. "Whether he knows it or not, one of these days he's going to be my husband."

"What do you mean, 'whether he knows it or not?'"

"Jamal wants to be a player, which I can understand. He's still young—29—and he likes to be out there in the world, you know what

I'm saying? It's like … um … it's like he's still trying to test himself and see what he can be, how he can make it."

"Is he acting like he's beginning to settle down?"

"I'd say a little. He still wants to be hard and hang out with his boys. Still goes to the go-go clubs all the time."

"Does he still mess around with other women?"

"Not that I know of. I think two babies in one year scared him a little. I don't think he's messing around still, but I can't say for certain that he's not."

"Don't you think you deserve to know?"

"I don't want to know. I just want to concentrate on taking care of my son, holding it together, and being patient. That's what my mother told me. I need to be patient."

"For Jamal, she means?"

"Yes, for Jamal. He and my mother get along great. She likes the way he takes care of the baby. My mother keeps him most days when I work and most of the time Jamal goes to pick him up, so he and my mother are always talking."

I quickly learn that Katrina's life as Jamal's lady-in-waiting involves more than mere doubt and disappointment. He controls all of the money in the household, including Katrina's small take-home pay from her job as a telemarketer, which is a part-time gig with no benefits. In fact, control appears to be an obsession with Katrina's boyfriend-cum-coparent-cum-prospective-groom. He dictates how Katrina should dress, with whom she associates, and where she goes. All the while, Jamal enjoys complete freedom.

"I almost never get to go out with him anymore because of the babysitter situation," Katrina explains. "When I go out with him, it's just too much drama. If I smile at some guy in the club, he says, 'Who was that?' and gets real mad. If I say I don't know, he tells me not to smile at dudes I don't know and make them think I'm interested in them. He says, 'Don't disrespect me.' That's his favorite saying."

"What if the man you smile at is a friend?"

"Oh, that's even worse, 'cause Jamal wants the whole story then. 'How do you know him? Did y'all ever go together? When's the last time he called you?' He's real possessive like that. One time I was talking to a friend of mine—a girl—and he stomps over and snatches my arm back, saying, 'You don't need to be with that ho' and 'that ho this' and 'that ho that.' It was so embarrassing. Everybody could hear it."

"What did you do when he did that?"

"Nothing. I just got real quiet, 'cause if I yelled back at him, he might hit me or something."

"Has he ever hit you?"

"No, but he would if I didn't just shut up. He'd probably take that as disrespecting him. He's weak, so weak."

"Then, no offense, Katrina, but why do you want him? I know what you said about the baby and all, but …"

"I love the man."

"You love someone who has a baby with another woman, who tells you what to wear, who scares you, and won't make any real commitment to you?"

"He is committed."

"How?"

"He comes to this house every night, no matter how late it is, no matter what the situation. This is where he comes. Deep down, I know Jamal loves me. He just has to grow up some more."

"Katrina, he's 29 years old. That's not old, but it's old enough, isn't it?"

"I guess not."

"So you're just going to wait it out?"

"Right."

"And stick it out, even though you're only 24 years old and you have a beautiful young son and a whole life ahead of you? You're going to wait for Jamal?"

"Like I said, I love him, and I know he loves me. If I just stay and wait and show him that I'm not one of these tricks that just wants to have a good time, if he sees that I love him enough to go through everything, we will be together and do that next thing."

"Marriage, you mean."

"Marriage. I know you don't think so, but it's gonna happen. You just wait."

. . .

Maybe it is love in the purest form. Unconditional love. Sacrificial love. Abiding, no-matter-what, 'til-death-do-us-part love. I suppose that's commendable. After all, even the best relationships have their ups and downs and their challenges, and no outsider, no matter how intimately connected he or she may be, can decode all of the messages and dynamics that transpire between two partners.

That said, I am at a loss to understand what's up with Felicia and Greg. In her early 30s, Felicia is an up-and-comer with a large defense contractor. She puts together some of the multimillion- or multibillion-dollar deals we hear so much about. Her job takes her to exotic locales regularly. When I talked to her, she had just returned from Tokyo.

Greg is one of those men that might have been a movie star if he hadn't been so good at corporate law. He spent his last year at Yale Law flipping through a stack of job offers. Some men have borderline good looks—no one finds them ugly, but not every woman finds them attractive either. Greg has the kind of looks that are universally appealing. Like most knockouts—male and female—he's well aware of his attributes.

"That swagger of his sickens me, to be honest," Felicia says. "I tease him about it all the time because he's so full of himself. But it works. It got me, didn't it? Of course, I have to remind him that I got him, too."

Felicia sounds happy at first. She seems to have accepted the fact that her boyfriend of five years has a Casanova-like air about him. But Greg doesn't reserve that charm just for the boardroom and his and Felicia's bedroom. He is, says Felicia, a chronic flirt and inveterate philander. There are other women she knows about; what worries her most are the ones she doesn't know about.

"He's as slick as they come," she says. "It would be one thing if he was cute and dumb, but Greg is very intelligent. He knows how to be discreet and he knows how to cover his bases. His problem is that I'm pretty smart myself, so I know about some of his sneaky shit."

"But you're still together."

"Greg has a way of making you forgive and forget. When I confronted him about the affairs—three times, no, wait, four, because one was actually a repeat—he acted afraid and ashamed that he was going to lose me. For a few days, I had all the power, you see. And I used that to my advantage."

"And after a few days?"

"I always break down. I can't take the puppy dog whimpering in the corner."

"Was it the same m.o. every time?"

"Pretty much. He fucks up, I find out, I get in his face, he does the puppy-dog thing, and I get soft. Then we start all over again until the next time."

"Are you hopeful about your relationship with Greg? Have things gotten better in that department?"

"Kind of. Not really. I don't know."

"But you're willing to put up with it, at least for now?"

Felicia clams up. A loud noise erupts in the background. "That was me kicking the trash can across the room," she says. "Damn."

"Are you okay?"

"Hell, no. What did I say yes to this interview for? No, I'm not all right, because I'm not feeling right about this shit, but I don't know what the hell to do. I don't know what to do." Felicia breaks down sobbing. I hadn't expected to touch such a nerve, and hadn't wanted to.

"Felicia, I'm sorry. We don't have to talk about this."

No response.

"Is there anything I can do? Are you all right?"

"I'm okay," she finally says. "And it wasn't you. I was thinking about this all the way home from Japan. A part of me knows that Greg is wrong for me. I deserve better than this. But I don't know how to do this thing right. I've tried ignoring it, I've tried beating him at his own game, I've tried confronting him, I've tried acting like I don't give a shit …"

"I know."

"But it's like he has me in some spell or something. And that's not me. That's not me to be so goddamn weak."

Felicia pauses. "I'm going to be all right. I just have to get a handle on this thing. I'm not making any excuses for Greg, but he does have all this temptation out there, and I think he's trying, I really do."

"And you believe he loves you."

"I believe that. Yes, I do. I know I love him."

Felicia was not the only self-avowed "sucker" on the line that day. I'm one of the world's biggest when it comes to good women with broken hearts.

"You hang in there," I say, sounding like a mama. "It's going to be all right."

"Okay, okay," Felicia says, sounding like a little girl. "I'm gonna go get myself together. Sorry about all this."

Me too.

· 12 ·

O Brothers, Where Art Thou?

C AN YOU IMAGINE what it must be like for Condoleezza Rice? Whatever you think of her politics, Dr. Rice's position as one of the most influential black women on the planet is unquestionable. Even if she became the mother of all Freestylers, don't you think she might have a hard time finding a love match?

As the United States Secretary of State, Dr. Rice is an expert at holding cards close to the vest, playing it cool, and being discriminating. Aside from the job, Condi Rice also appears to be a supremely private person. Therefore, many of us were surprised when she admitted to a reporter that she would like to have a boyfriend. Of course we weren't surprised that she was interested—just that she publicly acknowledged it.

The publicity may have helped. Or it may have been intended to throw nosy journalists off the trail of one man in particular—former San Francisco 49ers wide receiver Gene Washington. According to a friend, Condi and Gene met while he was an assistant athletic director at Stanford University and she was the prestigious school's provost: the youngest, the first black and the first female provost.

Good for her. Until Washington appeared on the scene, it seemed that Condoleezza Rice had a better shot at brokering Middle East peace than finding a compatible man. Some men may be put off by her conservative politics, but no one can doubt her smarts, her power, her cachet, her talent, or her class. She's all that, and pretty, too.

Assets aside, making a match for a single black woman with Condi

Rice's resumé is bound to be a hellish proposition. I'll bet the intimidation factor alone would wipe out a good two-thirds of potential boyfriends. Then there's the conversation conundrum. What do you say to grab and hold the attention of a woman who was dining with the king of Jordan the week before you picked her up for dinner and a movie? What does it take for a man to charm and amuse a woman who has watched the ballet from President Putin's gilded box at the Bolshoi and who has wowed world leaders from Rome to Tokyo, and London to Lagos?

There are some single black women who lead such extraordinary lives that there are practically no single black men in their peer group: important and exceptionally powerful women like Condoleezza Rice, and unbelievably rich women like Oprah Winfrey or a Washington media executive I know who is worth tens of millions, and maybe even a couple hundred million. I once asked her how many single black men she knew in her category. She leaned forward and smiled. "Zero."

It just goes to show you that power, money, and privilege aren't everything. They don't rub your feet, massage your shoulders, and ask if you're okay. They don't drop what they're doing and race across town to rescue you when your car runs out of gas. They don't brag about you to your friends, take you to meet their mothers, or treat your son to courtside seats at a game. They don't make you feel so good or so bad that you cry even though you're not the crying type. They may provide you with access to a president's ear, but the question is, who's whispering in yours?

We are rich, middle class, or poor; northerners, southerners, easterners, or westerners; young, middle-aged, or old; laden with degrees or studying for a G.E.D. But in some ways, we are all the same. The one thing that most single black women have in common is a wish that life could be a little bit sweeter. Often, one of the sugars we have in mind is a he. In some instances, he has a face and a name, but many cases, he is only a concept.

. . .

What do Sole Sisters want?

Research shows that black single women put more emphasis on background characteristics—social class, religion, race, and ethnicity—than white or Latino women, who focus more on the romantic notions of love, commitment, and fidelity. I doubt that it's as cut-and-dried as that suggests.

Background characteristics are used to narrow the attraction field. After all, one needs parameters. Common values are as good as any. Of course, inflexibility with your parameters is a problem, but no woman is going to bend if she doesn't have to.

Gigi (Shrinker): "I think pursuit of a man is complicated by values and desires—what a woman wants, and what she will not accept. The older I get, the less I'm willing to settle. I think most women feel the same."

Angie (Shrinker): "I want the companionship, the extra income, and a father figure for my daughters."

Michelle (Shrinker): "I really miss having a man when it snows and I have to shovel my own snow. You realize then that there's no one looking out for you."

Zena (Coaster): "Someone who makes you feel safe and secure. He is the joy-bringer, the love-giver, like Heather Headley sings."

. . .

What don't Sole Sisters want?

We can do without the stereotypes, thank you. We would like to be rid of the domineering woman, the sexually insatiable vixen, and the self-effacing, submissive servant-woman once and for all. We'd like to be allowed to assert ourselves without having to break through a wall of myths.

Vikki is a 32-year-old pharmaceutical sales representative in Alabama. Her last relationship ended five years ago, and it was "the last of a long string of fallen ones." She's on the lookout for a man to have a relationship with, but as she says, "I decided it was time for me to get myself together spiritually and emotionally. I am finally ready to move on and meet someone." Like most of the women I spoke with, Vikki resents it when people mistake willingness for desperation. "People are wrong if they think all single black women are desperate to find Mr. Right," she says.

The message is, "Brothers, relax." Not all single black women are stalking you and trying to lure you into the tall grasses. Not all of us are on standby to put you down or make you over. A lot of women enjoy giving as much as they enjoy receiving.

Linda (Shrinker): "I like having a companion, but I am learning to be comfortable being single."

Vanessa (Coaster): "I often wonder if the kind of relationship I'm envisioning is unrealistic. I'm just crazy enough to believe that two people can be committed, honest, caring, and unselfish. I understand now that my happiness is up to me, but I believe that two people can live their lives conscious of what needs to be done to keep a smile on the other person's face. I'd like to try."

Portia (Ticker): "I really get tired of people picking apart my whole life and saying, 'See, that's why you don't have a man,' or 'No wonder you're not married.' I think they're looking for something to be wrong with a black woman."

Linda (Shrinker): "Our men seem to prefer white, Asian, and Hispanic women—in that order—to black women."

Cecilia (Coaster): "Spontaneity is something that is hard for men to accept from women. If you come up with something all of a sudden, it's rare for you to get a positive response. I think there's a control issue. It's really unfortunate, too, because that power struggle is just a manifestation of insecurity. When you haven't been loved—and a lot of these men have not been loved—there's a big hole there. The insecurity is going to surface over and over again."

Camille (Swingle): "It's so simple. I want a man who enjoys being happy. I don't mean just someone who is happy when I meet him, but one who actually enjoys it, and one that will love me, and allow me to love him back. One who trusts love."

· · ·

There's a clever cartoon about the single life that is making the e-mail rounds. I've gotten copies from at least 10 friends, all of whom are single black women like me. The drawing features five cobweb-shrouded skeletons seated around a dusty dining table. The caption says something along the lines of "women waiting for Mr. Right."

We Sole Sisters tend to laugh at ourselves a lot. Humor is a valuable piece of equipment in our arsenal of coping skills. We laugh about our misadventures in dating. We laugh about our friends and relatives' matchmaking attempts. We laugh at our sometimes expensive and often uncomfortable efforts to look like a million dollars while pretending it's effortless. We laugh at the tired old lines, the antics, and the mind games played both on us and by us. We laugh at the absurdity and redundancy of our aloneness, and about all of those Friday nights spent with takeout and nature shows.

But for untold numbers of single black women who would prefer to have a solid relationship with a man than to go it alone—millions, maybe—there's not much that's funny about the absence of a man that fits their needs. For some it's not just a challenge, but also a dilemma—particularly for those Sole Sisters for whom a love connection is a priority.

It is also a threat to the posterity of black America. Declining courtships threaten the marriage rate, the birth rate, the prosperity of black households, and the social and perhaps emotional development of children—in other words, the well-being of black America.

Sounds like a crisis to me.

Even in times of slavery, when black life was most degraded, men and women found a way to make and maintain monogamous commitments. As historian Jacqueline Jones wrote in *Labor of Love, Labor of Sorrow: Black Women, Work, and the Family from Slavery to the Present*: "For young black people of both sexes, courtship was both a diversion and delight. The ritual itself appears to have been intensely romantic, with compatibility and physical attraction the primary considerations." Jones gives examples of rivalries among men competing for a particular young woman. She quotes the recollections of former slaves who knew girls that played "coy and 'hard to get.'" During this era, black marriages were not legally recognized, but slaves and ex-slaves honored tradition nonetheless and upheld the spirit of monogamous, committed love … even if the law refused to see it.

Have black men and women lost the capacity to connect? Of course not. But "coy and 'hard to get'" are rare tactics these days. If you understand how men tick, the black woman-black man relationship is bound to have been damaged by the eagerness of so many women to give or share the things that were once reserved only for men who pledged—and to varying degrees, proved—their love and fidelity. Doing so shortchanges men by denying them the sublime joy of proving their worthiness.

There's another, much more insidious culprit. The constant drip, drip, drip of racism and bigotry and the discriminatory policies, laws, and practices that they spawn have a corrosive effect on black relationships. Black women still have to wrestle with the mammy (subservient), Jezebel (promiscuous), and Sapphire (shrewish) stereotypes. Black men are still miscast as oversexed, ambitionless, and violent. These obscene stereotypes are often embedded in law and policy, and sometimes they even have monuments—like the proliferation of prisons. Part of the reason the prison industry is going gangbusters today is because society expects, and is preparing a place for, endless waves of allegedly incorrigible, dangerous, and ultimately disposable black men. Imagine what that does to a brother's psyche.

Verily, in the quest for functional, monogamous relationships, there are many mountains to climb.

"There's nothing in our DNA. There's nothing deficient about us," said sociologist Donna L. Franklin in an interview with Denver's *Rocky Mountain News*. "Any group that's been through what we've been through—slavery, the economic marginalization of black men which has forced black women in[to] the marketplace, being stigmatized by color—would be experiencing the same problems we are."

Dr. Franklin is so right. It's not DNA; it's circumstances.

. . .

What about us? What about the millions of single black women who would like to do our part to propagate the race, support traditions, and get some soul satisfaction, but are having little luck, bad luck, or no luck in making the necessary connections. What do we do?

Obviously, social activism and political agitation are sorely needed. Attitudes, policy, law, customs … all have to change in order to reverse the troubling trend.

But unless there are some good prospects at the rally or in the picket line (and there could be), I doubt that's what most Sole Sisters want to hear right now. Saturday night is coming soon. O Brothers, where art thou?

· 13 ·

You Don't Know Me Like That!

M Y YOUNG FRIEND, CAMILLE—she of the instant messages— had one point that bears examination in any discussion of the man-woman dilemma in black America. "I get tired of black men saying that we are angry black women," she wrote. It's a recurring complaint among black women.

The Angry Black Woman image weaves in and out of our history. Legend defines us with negative blurbs: in-your-face, no-holds-barred, take-no-prisoners, cuss-you-out, kick-your-ass, cut-you-loose, bust-your-balls, pack-your-shit, damn-your-mama, hit-the-road, and bring-it-on. Supposedly, that's what we're about: hard, tough, and mad at the world. Our constant battle with this stereotype sometimes leads us to live it. Being portrayed as angry all the time is going to make you angry sometimes.

When black men fling that accusation at us, the anger is usually a symptom of another emotion—hurt. We expect them to understand, to figure us out, and to know why we handle things as we do. Instead, they often contribute to the denigration of black women as domineering, gold-digging, overly materialistic, and sexually manipulative.

. . .

"This woman I know just wants somebody to help her pay her bills," claims Jawan, 28, who works for an overnight delivery service.

"Why do you say that?" I ask.

"It's obvious," he says. "She has all these shoes—more shoes than a shoe store—and she has expensive jewelry."

"How did she get them?"

"She bought 'em. She's always shopping, shopping, shopping."

"But she pays for them herself?"

"Yeah."

"Has she ever asked you to buy shoes, or jewelry, or anything else for her?"

"Not in so many words. But you know she can't keep doing all that shopping and pay her normal bills forever. She's going to need some help so she can keep up that style of life."

"Did she say that?"

"Naw, not in so many words. But you can put two and two together."

"And what do you like to buy with your money?"

"Me, I'm a simple man. I like music—CDs and stuff. Sometimes I buy a sweater or a pair of pants, but I try to save. For a rainy day, you know."

"Ever think that you could buy more CDs and sweaters or save more if you combined incomes with someone else?"

"I know what you're trying to say, but it's not like that, you know? She'd go through her money and mine."

"You know this."

"I know this. I've seen how she spends."

"How does she love you? Good?"

"Aw, yeah. She's a real sweet woman, and she's real good to me."

"But you won't commit to her because you think she wants your money."

"Aw, don't say it like that. I'm not saying that."

"Then what are you saying?"

Jawan had no answer.

It was not my place to tell him how to run his life, but I hope I gave him something to think about. By his own account, his girlfriend is good to him, and he professes love for her. But an assumption has blocked his view. He does not see her clearly or fully. He presumes that because she likes to spend the money she makes, she will spend the money he makes just as freely, and even recklessly. They've got a relationship that could be redeemed and secured by two things: a good conversation, and a good plan.

. . .

Then there's Rob, who suffers from what I call the "Beyonce Syndrome." He believes that no matter how good the woman in his life is, there's a superstar out there for him somewhere, just waiting to be discovered. Somewhere, there's a dream girl, as beautiful, talented, sexy, nice, and rich as the world-famous singer and actress who, along with Jennifer Lopez, made the round, fleshy booty an asset rather than a liability in the attraction ledger.

Rob's girl, Tasha, is a brown-skinned lovely with mesmerizing eyes and a near-perfect figure. She is a medical transcriptionist who drives a nice car, works out three days a week, sings in her church's choir, regularly attends her book club meetings, is known to make a "killer" beef brisket and "perfect" mashed potatoes, and is adored by her family. Rob calls her "the best," and he's been with her—and her only, he swears—for four years.

Both Rob and Tasha are 30. She wants to get married, have a couple of years as just a couple, and then have children. Her appeals for a trip to the altar become more frequent and more urgent, Rob says. He says she's the love of his life. But he won't make that move.

"Do you just not want to be married?" I ask.

"Oh, no, it's not that. I want to be a family man someday."

"Some day, but not *to*day," I say. "And not tomorrow either, huh?"

Rob laughs nervously. "Not tomorrow, but not too long."

"What will it take to make that happen?" I ask him.

"I don't know. Just more time."

"And what will more time give you?"

"It'll just let me be sure that Tasha and I are meant to be. I want to be sure because I only want to do this one time. Then it's forever."

"That's commendable. But after four years, don't you know if you and Tasha are meant to be?"

"Pretty much. But I want to make sure."

"And how do you do that?"

He fidgets.

"Rob?"

"I'm trying to think of how to put this. It's like … I don't know how to say this. I don't want to do the wedding thing and the buy-the-house thing and the have-the-babies thing and then, boom, find out that I'm really not happy with the situation."

"So you want a sure thing? A guarantee?"

"No, I'm not talking about a guarantee. I don't expect that. But it's a big world out there. You know what I'm saying? There are millions of women out there."

"So you need to meet a few more million before you know."

"Aw, no! A few more million. Dang, I'm not trying to be a player. I'm not a player. I just want to be right about this."

"But you have this beautiful, intelligent, devoted, and good woman already."

"Right."

"You know what they say about a 'bird in the hand'? You're going to take the chance of losing Tasha because there might be someone else out there who is beautiful, intelligent, devoted, and good?"

"I see what you're saying. But it's not like that. I just want to be sure. I don't know how to put what I'm trying to say."

"You want Beyonce, right?"

"I want Beyonce?"

"You're looking for the superstar woman?"

"Um, not that. I'm looking for my superstar, not necessarily the world's superstar. Not necessarily a woman that the whole world loves."

"But someone who's more than Tasha."

"Naw, Tasha, she's got it all."

"Then, I go back to question one: What are you waiting for?"

"That's a good question, I guess. I can't really explain it. I'm just not ready."

Such is the mystery that confounds us all. When a man has a woman he loves and who loves him, who he satisfies and who satisfies him, with whom he's compatible, who he knows and who knows him, what is he waiting for? Come on, brother. Do you really need it to be more bootylicious than that?

I must tell you that I'm happy for the many women who are content to have no man in their lives. They are inspirations and role models to us all. They're paragons of independence, self-respect, strength, and discipline. They remind us that life is what you make of it, and that in any construct, life can be pleasurable and fulfilling.

But I ache for women with so much love to give, and no willing or competent receiver. It is a terrible waste of goodness. It is a terrible waste of opportunity for joy, pleasure, security, and well being. It is children unborn, homes unfurnished, memories unmade, legacies unformed, and history unwritten. Some of life goes undone only because of misunderstandings, a lack of communication, snap judgments, or silly fears.

The hearts of men and women alike deserve so much better.

· 14 ·

Getting Real, Getting Healed

IN THE END, there's only so much a cozy blanket, a good TV show, and a big bowl of butter pecan ice cream can do for a girl. They suffice on many lonesome nights, but not all of them. Sometimes—especially on sultry summer nights and breezy fall evenings and clear spring dusks and cold winter evenings and Sunday through Saturday—you want more.

For some women, a fellow sprawled across the sofa with one hand on the remote and the other in his waistband will do, but most of us want romance. Some of us just would like the promise of it. The possibility of it. A bit of assurance that one day soon, or right now, if we'd like, there will be dazzle in our nights beyond fleece coverlets, warring lions and hyenas, and pints of fattening goodness from Baskin-Robbins. One of these days, there will be a man who makes us laugh and who can handle the little girl, the vixen, the bitch on wheels, the sophisticate, the domestic goddess, the careerist—all that we are. A man who is a friend, defender, confidante, partner, and lover. A man who gets us, and who adores what others might find strange or annoying. A man who shows up, and calls, and contributes and assists when he says that he will. A man who is only interested in us and makes life just a little bit sweeter when he's around. That's the dream that keeps us going.

Black women are traditionally problem solvers. We are resilient, resourceful, and determined. We are gifted with a strong survival instinct, and we have mastered coping skills that speak as much to our hopefulness as to our resolve. We are faithful to the ideas of love, passion, security, sharing, and joy.

But how do we fix this problem? Have we at long last come up against an unconquerable challenge? After all, this is a basic supply-side issue; we can't go back in time and make more black men, keep them healthy and alive, get them educated, and prepare them for this surplus of women. We can't raise our dead brothers from the grave; break our incarcerated brothers out of prison; cure the sick and addicted brothers; clean out the heads of all the brothers who are messed up by racism, abuse, and lousy upbringing; or get the aimless brothers up to speed in time to meet the demand.

There is plenty of advice out there on this subject, and much of it, of course, is for sale. Some of it appears as formulas, strategies, or checklists for finding, winning, and keeping Mr. Right.

In these times, there are temptations to resort to unconventional means. The proliferation of online dating services, the advent of speed dating, and the ubiquity of singles bars and "meat markets" attest to the growing market of singles on the make. One beautiful, statuesque orthodontist I know pays $100 a month for a membership in a matchmaking service. She was having no luck "on the scene." She has yet to find a match through the service, but she's willing to give it six more months. "After that, I guess I'll just give up," she says.

Don't tell this woman that she needs to compromise or, to put it more gloomily, to "settle." Turning her personal life over to a bank of strangers *is* settling, in her opinion. She's already made a concession in her method of finding a mate, so she doesn't want to compromise her standards when it comes to the kind of man she is looking for. That, she says, would not be settling. That would be selling out. "I'd rather be alone," she says.

On the other hand, as we have seen, there are women in such dire and pathetic need for a male companion that all they require is a Y chromosome. I don't think that's most of us. I hope it's not many of us.

God bless the legion that is at peace with their mateless states. Even if they're not at peace, at least they're not hysterical. Pardon my presumptuousness, but while it is entirely possible to lead a happy and fulfilling life alone, most of us single women would rather not.

All is not lost. Dr. Brenda Wall, a psychologist and relationship expert, offers some balm to soothe our wounded, broken, or lovelorn hearts. It's palatable advice, but no guarantee. Dr. Wall's opinions, cautions, encouragement and admonitions vary from type to type.

Shrinkers. "Resilient black women always are able to find experiences that allow them to flourish and be successful. You have a wonderful relationship with your kids. You have work that is gratifying. You have accomplishments, and maybe acclaim.

"Because you're so effective in that area, you aren't looking in other areas because that may be a place that you haven't done the healing. The strength is that you're okay, and the downside is that there's a place in you that is just as special and wonderful that is not being tended to because that may be a place where you have unresolved healing.

"Two things will happen: You will get to a place where you go after that, or God will put you in a place where you have to go after that."

Freestylers. "If a sister says she's throwing the rules out, what she's really expressing is either an unhealthy or healthy description about herself. If she's throwing the rules out [and lowering her standards], that's probably a function of self-destruction. However, if she is aware that her rules are different from society's rules, and what she looks at is heart and character, then she's not throwing the rules out. She's operating by a different set of rules.

"In the name of throwing away the rules, [some] women act out of desperation or act out of a need for control. They lower their standards and boast about doing so. Either is unhealthy.

"If we look at ourselves in terms of African-American people—if we go back two generations—the rules were different. Men and women knew how to build relationships based on strength. It was not uncommon to find a schoolteacher married to a man engaged in manual labor. She was addressing a 'rule' that was built on [the] standards of building a family and a community. Together, they educated one another. There was never embarrassment.

"Our wonderful parents gave us an opportunity to go through doors that [they] couldn't, and we went crazy. They didn't realize that we would abandon the value system and replace it with someone else's 'rules.'"

Swingles. "If you're truly happy with this free-wheeling lifestyle, fine. But you need to make sure you're dealing with your own questions about sexual morality, health, and spiritual and emotional prerequisites. What are the implications of what you're doing?

"Even if you're handling what you call fun, can the other people in your world handle it? Can your children? Can the person with whom you're partying?

"The Swingle needs to ask herself: Is this sexual involvement that someone else is defining? Is it that someone else is really having all the fun at your expense? Is it a sexual exploitation in a subtle way? Are there a mood-altering substances involved? Follow the worry to where it takes you.

"Chances are, if there's a worry, it's a reality. There's a part of you that recognizes that you are not acting in your own best interest, and that you are replacing your capacity for depth with a distraction for entertainment."

Tickers. "Instead of trusting their own strength, they see themselves in terms of what's missing. Instead of trusting the choices they may have made—their decisions to continue with school, walk out of a bad relationship, advance their careers—they're giving up on themselves and listening to a negative voice. That becomes an excuse for lowering standards."

Naw Naws. "Part of what you want to say to them—if they have really made up their minds [not to get involved with a man]—is, 'Is this necessary to keep you safe?' If this is what they choose, fine.

"But sometimes, the protection may be so deeply rooted that you don't see it that way. Make sure that you are so happy with yourself that you really are okay. Women can be healthy, whole, and wonderful outside a relationship. They can be 20 and make that choice; they can be 70 and make that choice. When people ask,

'What's wrong with you?' they know if that's coming from genuine interest or envy.

"If she's really adamant, it's sometimes a cover. But it's all right to be where you are and be balanced. It's important to know that when people are asking you questions, sometimes it's because they care, and sometimes not."

Coasters. "If you're really coasting, then you're going to have experiences when you would have some moments [with men] and other times when you are not because there is so much else going on in your life to keep you occupied. If you're really all right inside, I think it's okay to be holier-than-thou. You want to celebrate where you are. You compare yourself to other people as a way of feeling better about yourself. That's not really healthy, but it's okay, because these are ways with coping with where you are. Some of it's healthy and some of it's not."

Double Dippers. "In spite of what you have, you're demonstrating an inability to be available to yourself. If you're capable of being available to yourself, the quality of the relationship you have with another person is going to honor you and him. Double Dippers do neither. They live in a world where there is no honor and no respect, and there's going to be a lot of conflict. Instead of facing the conflict, they cover it with people.

"The issue is the great damage that they do to themselves. It's so common; it doesn't look like it's destructive. But look across the community and see that a broken family produces very troubled children. Go to any school and talk to the children, who are so fragile. There is no recognition of responsibility to oneself, and since that's missing, there is an inability to have a responsibility to another adult.

"We don't care that she's taking someone else's man. Both of them would be involved in pathological relationships because the person that she's involved with has a reciprocal inability to deal with the wonderful human issues facing adulthood. They're both losers, in effect. It's a very selfish relationship, and there's no responsibility in it. They aren't getting together to talk about the revolution; they aren't talking about the Second Coming. They aren't talking about preparing their children to read."

Flamekeepers. "For people who have not fully developed themselves, it may be easier to keep a flame than develop an authentic relationship. This becomes a nice way of hiding the fact that there is an inability to handle adult intimacy.

"The Flamekeeper is unavailable for a quality life. But a woman honoring a love that is gone but was good is not a Flamekeeper; she is a relationship-keeper. And that is fine, unless the past relationship is an obstacle to a fulfilling future one.

"I once met a wonderful man whose wife had died after quite an ordeal with breast cancer. I asked, 'Did you mess around?' He said, 'Of course not. We did everything we could to keep her living as long as we could.' It wasn't that the sick person was a burden. The sick person was a person, and the relationship was still there. You don't keep the flame, you keep the relationship. You maintain that wholesome relationship with a person.

"But most of the time, when people tell me they're waiting for someone or holding onto someone who is not available, they're the ones who are unavailable for an adult relationship. They're living their lives in a different way."

Knitters. "If you're in a relationship that's working for you, you're not going to be haunted. You're going to love your partner enough to know if your partner could and should be with you. You're going to be very aware of where you are in the relationship. If that's not happening—if you can't gauge where you are—you know it.

"The issue is not about confronting him [about where the relationship is headed], it's about confronting yourself. If you're saying, 'I know he's not going to marry me, but I'm not interested in looking because the sex is good and the fun is good,' you've got to confront your truth if you want to stop knitting and be happy."

Trippers. "The other person is just as messed up as you are. So it's easy to hate a violent perpetrator than it is to recognize, my gosh, they are both mirrors of one pain. What you do is help a person deal with herself. You want to remove the pain. The pain serves a purpose. It is part of identity.

"The woman is telling herself, '[One of two] things has to happen: Either I have to torture myself, or someone else has to torture me.' I think what's important is that as long as you are willing to lose your identity, other people will pretend that you aren't there.

"In abusive relationships, healing [must] takes place. There's got to be a point where degradation, destruction, and damage no longer have a place in your life. When you outgrow it, it's easy to exit.

"We live in such a violent world in the United States. There is such a low view of women that it is very hard to [raise] vibrant, wonderful daughters who grow into contributing, lovely women. There's great anger. And the anger results in some great barriers."

. . .

Let me say it once more: Although it has frightening implications for the survival of the black family as we have known it, the trend toward singlehood for black women is, for many of us, more of a situation than a problem.

Dr. Wall underscores this point. "Black women have tremendous spiritual and emotional power that is hidden because they're so busy doing miraculous work—the children we rear, the racism we endure, the men we replace. There is great hidden talent that gets relabeled, usually as something negative. We participate in some of that ourselves," she notes.

"We haven't dealt with the sexual abuse that is a legacy of slavery. Now we have all this that is taking us away from community healing, because we see ourselves as apart," she continues. "And we take on the language of the oppressor, the thoughts of the oppressor. Consequently, we don't hold hands with each other. We don't take care of each other."

Permit this righteous sister to roll. Attitude is a large part of what ails us.

"What you hear black women say is, 'We know we live in a world where our men have been under assault, and we haven't done anything about it,'" Dr. Wall says. "Look at the number of men who are locked up. I think that's because we have not addressed the problems directly. We allow ourselves to say that the men are beneath us. Quite frankly, our men are available and wonderful, but we generally are ill equipped to connect with the power. So, we connect with our own pain, which has to do with our inadequacy—even though we say that we are dealing with their inadequacy. We need to develop intimacy with men who can show us who we really are."

For those of us who have been hurt, neglected, or rejected by black men, Dr. Wall sees a lot of healing work to be done. For one thing, she says, "If we have had failed experiences with men who have not been able to do what they say they could have, we should be the generation that produced well-adjusted, loving men." Instead, she laments, some of us fail to raise our sons in a way that would be fair and honorable to the women they will grow up to love—as if we want to be the only woman to ever really command their devotion and respect.

"Part of what has happened is that even though we may have a church experience, we can look at a good relationship [with a man] and have no concept of what a *godly* relationship is about.

"Tapping into the spiritual works. Most religious women would say that ... healthy women build those relationships.

"You have to come to a decision about spiritual identity. As brilliant as we are, most of us know when we have a piece of unhealed work we are not dealing with. We know that we are still sensitive about the fact that our father was not there, or that our mother was not there. We know that there is one thing that, if it is faced, will free us to be the women we were created to be.

"We have not taken the opportunity to address the problems before us that can be solved. We can address white supremacy, illiteracy, and drugs in our community. Instead, we coexist with them. As long as we coexist with such huge community problems, it's going to affect our relationships.

"As long as we allow unquestioned evil to thrive in our world, it will affect us. That would be why we have disproportionate relationships between men and women, and disproportionate distributions of wealth.

"If we are the women who have been wronged, it need not be in vain. We should be the women who ensure that the next generation will be balanced. We should be able to put a value system in place that protects our daughters."

Certainly it is worth the effort to give our sons and daughters the opportunity we didn't have, failed to recognize, couldn't find, took for granted, or couldn't see for the trees. It is cold comfort in those moments when we want this one thing—a satisfying relationship—just for ourselves. But it is some comfort.

And I'll bet the afterglow is pretty good.